Praise for Alejandro Jodorowsky and His Works

"Jodorowsky is a brilliant, wise, gentle, and cunning wizard with tremendous depth of imagination and crystalline insight into the human condition."

DANIEL PINCHBECK, AUTHOR OF
BREAKING OPEN THE HEAD

"Alejandro Jodorowsky seamlessly and effortlessly weaves together the worlds of art, the confined social structure, and things we can only touch with an open heart and mind."

ERYKAH BADU, ARTIST AND ALCHEMIST

"One of the most inspiring artists of our time. . . . A prophet of creativity."

KANYE WEST, RECORDING ARTIST

"*The Dance of Reality* begs to be read as a culminating work. . . ."

LOS ANGELES TIMES

"*The Dance of Reality* [film] is a trippy but big-hearted reimagining of the young Alejandro's unhappy childhood in a Chilean town. . . ."

NEW YORK TIMES MAGAZINE

"*Manual of Psychomagic* is great . . . like a cookbook of very useful recipes that can help us to understand our life and the universe we live in."

MARINA ABRAMOVIĆ, PERFORMANCE ARTIST

"His films *El Topo* and *The Holy Mountain* were trippy, perverse, and blasphemous."

WALL STREET JOURNAL

"The best movie director ever!"

MARILYN MANSON, MUSICIAN, ACTOR,
AND MULTIMEDIA ARTIST

Sacred Trickery
and the Way of Kindness
The Radical Wisdom of Jodo

Alejandro Jodorowsky
with Gilles Farcet

Translated by Ariel Godwin

Inner Traditions
Rochester, Vermont • Toronto, Canada

Inner Traditions
One Park Street
Rochester, Vermont 05767
www.InnerTraditions.com

SUSTAINABLE FORESTRY INITIATIVE   Certified Sourcing
www.sfiprogram.org
SFI-00854

Text stock is SFI certified

Originally published in French under the title *La Tricherie sacrée: Entretiens avec Gilles Farcet* by Éditions Dervy
First U.S. edition published in 2016 by Inner Traditions

Library of Congress Cataloging-in-Publication Data
Names: Jodorowsky, Alejandro, interviewee. | Farcet, Gilles, 1959– interviewer. | Godwin, Ariel, translator.
Title: Sacred trickery and the way of kindness : the radical wisdom of Jodo / Alejandro Jodorowsky and Gilles Farcet ; translated by Ariel Godwin.
Other titles: Tricherie sacrâee. English
Description: First U.S. edition. | Rochester, Vermont : Inner Traditions, 2016. | Includes index. | "Originally published in French under the title La Tricherie sacrâee: Entretiens avec Gilles Farcet, by âEditions Dervy."
Identifiers: LCCN 2015027312| ISBN 9781620554593 (paperback) | ISBN9781620554609 (e-book)
Subjects: LCSH: Jodorowsky, Alejandro—Philosophy. | Jodorowsky, Alejandro—Interviews. | BISAC: BODY, MIND & SPIRIT / Inspiration & Personal Growth. | BIOGRAPHY & AUTOBIOGRAPHY / Personal Memoirs. | PHILOSOPHY / Metaphysics.
Classification: LCC PQ7298.2.O3 Z46 2016 | DDC 868/.6409—dc23
LC record available at http://lccn.loc.gov/2015027312

Printed and bound in the United States by Lake Book Manufacturing, Inc. The text stock is SFI certified. The Sustainable Forestry Initiative® program promotes sustainable forest management.

10 9 8 7 6 5 4 3 2 1

Text design and layout by Debbie Glogover
This book was typeset in Garamond Premier Pro with Copperplate Gothic, Gill Sans, and Avenir as display fonts

Inner Traditions wishes to express its appreciation for assistance given by the government of France through the National Book Office of the Ministère de la Culture in the preparation of this translation.

Nous tenons à exprimer nos plus vifs remerciements au gouvernement de la France et au ministère de la Culture, Centre National du Livre, pour leur concours dans la préparation de la traduction de cet ouvrage.

CONTENTS

PART THREE

ONCE THERE WAS JODO:
TESTIMONIES

INTRODUCTION

TRICKERY, FIFTEEN YEARS LATER
By Gilles Farcet

In 1989 Dervy published *La Tricherie sacrée,* a small volume of spontaneous conversations between Alejandro Jodorowsky and myself. This little book had a surprising destiny: without causing any hubbub, it continued to attract new readers over the years. "Jodo" already had a solid reputation as a storyline writer of *bandes dessinées,* which he insisted on calling by their American name, "comics."* He was also known in France, his adopted country, as well as on the other side of the Atlantic, as a director of pioneering cult films. He was less well known as a free and brilliant spiritual maverick.

A free and brilliant maverick indeed, for how can one

---

*[The French term *bandes dessinées* (literally: drawn strips) has no exact equivalent in English. "Comics" implies humorous content, which is not always present. "Graphic novel" implies a continuous, novel-like storyline, which is not always the case. Therefore, the French term (sometimes abbreviated BD) is used throughout this translation. —Trans.]

describe this man? A tarologist? But he is more than that, even though the consultations one finds advertised today in numerous trendy coffee shops have their origins in his "Mystic Cabaret" and in many cases are offered by his disciples. Spiritual master? Even though he sometimes likes to describe himself as a "poor guru exploited by the spiritual business," Jodo is not and does not pretend to be a "master" in the traditional sense of the term. He does not fit into any specific tradition, even though he often makes reference to the masters who crossed his path, notably the Zen roshi Ejo Takata, the sorceress Pachita, and the mysterious Castaneda. As he has explained in our more recent conversations, when he believes that someone who has come to consult with him needs contact with a spiritual master, he directs her toward Arnaud Desjardins, because Jodorowsky does not see himself as proposing a path. An extraordinary esotericist? A healer always ready to pull a "psychomagical act" out of his hat? An atypical sorcerer? A transcendental illusionist? A sublime charlatan? In truth, regarding his spiritual life, as in all other aspects of his incredibly rich life, Jodorowsky is a being outside of the norm, one of those people whose very existence is an initiatory saga.

However abundant and varied his creativity may be, it is supported by an inner life, a truly spiritual journey. And the present book was the first significant account of that journey. Coming about as a small miracle, this book, conceived of when its subject had just reached the age of sixty, inaugurated a new era for him. While still pursuing his artistic activities—essentially the "comics"—he became increasingly known among certain people in his role as a "magus," much like Gurdjieff in his time, with whom Jodorowsky shares the distinction of having influenced numerous artists, as the testimonies in the third part of this book will show.

La Tricherie was also the prelude to another book, *Le Théâtre de la guérison,* in which Alejandro developed his "psychomagical" vision.

Here I would like to share some memories from the era following the publication of *La Tricherie.*

I saw Alejandro and Arnaud Desjardins again on the occasion of their first meeting together, at my residence in Paris. I remember Arnaud as his familiar self—curious—as a producer, to meet another filmmaker, and interested, as a disciple of the way—for although he acted as master, Arnaud lived above all as a disciple—to meet this unusual person whose depths he had become aware of through the reading of *La Tricherie.* And I remember Alejandro starting out sincerely shy, retreating into a corner at the beginning of the evening, wearing his purple suit, repeating in a candid tone: "I am so in awe to meet such a person as Arnaud, I am only a poor man, what inestimable luck for a poor man like me . . ."

The ice melted very quickly, and the timidity gave way to a very eloquent Jodo and an Arnaud radiating contentment. The former embarked upon a long discussion, as incomprehensible as it was fascinating, on the subject of the Ninja Turtles—in which, at the time, he saw as an esoteric saga ("You understand, all explanations of the world today come down to the Ninja Turtles")—as well as his memories of David Carradine, the *Kung Fu* hero, giving a stunning demonstration of karate in his living room in Los Angeles, finally returning to his magical encounter with Castaneda.

When I met Arnaud at his publisher's the next morning,

he—who was always so measured, prudent, and difficult to impress, even when rubbing shoulders with some of the biggest spiritual names of the century—said to me, with a childlike smile, "Now I've slept on it, I admit it: I am amazed by this Jodorowsky . . ."

This was the beginning of a relationship of mutual respect. As Alejandro likes to say, they recognized one another mutually in their honesty.

And while we are on the subject of spiritual guides, I also remember a day in April 1992 when Lee Lozowick arrived. He was an American rock singer, relatively well known in France today, but at the time totally unknown.

As soon as he got off the plane from Arizona, on his first stay in France (which I had organized), he declared with a resolute air: "I don't want to relax. No rest! I want action!"

Because people at the end of a fourteen-hour trip involving a time change generally prefer a gentle beginning for their visit, I thought I had done well not to plan anything in particular for that first evening. What, then, could I suggest? How to improvise a fun time for a frenetic American guru and his entourage (for he was traveling with about ten people, his students, family, friends)? And then the obvious solution suddenly presented itself. Jodo! What other person could I call on the spur of the moment to entertain a clan of American shamanic rock disciples?

"Hello, Alejandro?"

"Good evening. . . . An American guru? Bring them all over; I'll be expecting you at my place . . ."

So it was that Lee and his entourage headed for the suburb of Vincennes and spent their first evening in Paris in very creative company, for besides the master of the house, we found there none other than Mœbius and Boucq, two masters of "comics" reunited with their scriptwriter, mentor, and friend. We all sat around on cushions in a room of the house and improvised a sort of spontaneous workshop, led by Jodo with great verve in an English that was as fluent and melodious as his French. Each person talked about his practices, his manner of working, until Alejandro delivered the conclusion with his typical serious humor: "The problem is, we all agree!" The evening ended with Mœbius and Boucq each hunched over a piece of paper on the floor, working on drawings for Lee. These drawings can be seen today, hanging in the refectory of his ashram in Arizona.

During this period I also remember beginning to panic when I found that Jodo appeared not to know how to follow a schedule and wrote nothing down. When we had to be at public engagements, this led to situations that were disconcerting but, in the end, always instructive. Later he relied on his partner, Marianne, to help him keep his appointments, but at that time he had no stable companion to look out for him. As a consequence I was left with the task of calming down an auditorium full of several hundred people who had come to see him and of tracking down Jodo—who had simply forgotten—while praying that he had not fled to Mexico or embarked on some other adventure.

A few more jumbled images: Jodo consulting his magnificent notebook of dreams, an enormous colored volume in which he wrote them down, and a letter suddenly falling out of it, which, when I picked it up, turned out to be from John Lennon . . .

Jodo at the Marjolaine, getting up in front of a conference room full of people who had come, due to an error in the program, to hear Dr. Woestlandt, and declaring royally: "Listen . . . I am not the Dr. Westphaler whom you have come to see. But the person is of no importance. I did not want to come to the Marjolaine, but I am here. So because I am here, pretend that I am Dr. Wiesen-Wiesen and ask me your questions. I will answer as if I were Dr. Woof-Woof . . ."

What could have been relatively disastrous ended in triumph, with Jodo tearing himself away from a crowd of new admirers in order to search for the stand where he could find the book written by the person the audience had originally come to see: "In any case, I will buy the book of this Doctor Westphallus . . ."

Jodo publicly breaking all the rules of the spiritually correct and improvising a psychomagical act to teach a lesson to a conference organizer whom he considered greedy—see the story he tells in our interviews. Jodo telling dirty jokes and extracting esoteric meaning from them—see his book *La Sagesse des blagues* (The Wisdom of Jokes).

Jodo presiding over his "Mystic Cabaret" in front of an auditorium packed with aficionados who had come, drawn solely by word of mouth, to participate in this free weekly workshop . . .

I am certain of one thing: whatever the many and sometimes disturbing facets of his personality, Jodorowsky is a good man, kind and brilliant, driven by generous intentions.

The 2004 edition of *La Tricherie sacrée* is an expanded version of the little book that was published in 1989 and is organized as follows:

First following this preface is the unaltered main text of the 1989 edition, including the original preface and the brief postscript. This is followed by a new, briefer dialogue between us, where we catch up with each other fifteen years later. Finally the third section of this new edition consists of testimonies from four very different personalities, their common factor being that they were marked, in some way or another, by their encounter with Jodorowsky. For this I thank Philippe Manœuvre, Coralie Trin Thi, François Boucq, and Arnaud Desjardins, who kindly shared some time with me in order to pay homage to Jodo. I believe that these testimonies allow for a better glimpse into the dimension and universality of his personality.

I am grateful also for the confidences of one of his three living sons, Adan.

Finally there is a Jodorowskian pirouette in which the interviewer becomes the interviewee.

I would like to thank Lila Faure for her excellent work in recapturing the text of the first edition and Éditions Dervy for breathing new life into *La Tricherie*.

Let the party go on!

GILLES FARCET
CHARMES, JANUARY 2004

PART ONE

Sacred Trickery
1989

ONE

UNDER JODO'S SUN

It was many years ago that I first viewed Alejandro Jodorowsky with admiration, tinged with fear . . .

I must have been seventeen years old when a substantial article in *Rock & Folk* made me aware of the existence on this planet of a madman determined to put the world of Frank Herbert's initiatory novel, *Dune,* onto film. For that purpose this maniac was associating with another demented demiurge, the artist Mœbius, otherwise Jean Giraud, whose adventures of Lieutenant Blueberry had marked the lost prairie of my childhood. Those first years, passing so slowly, leading unbeknownst toward the crevice of adolescence, remain forever like a Far West of my soul.

I was seventeen, then, and aching to rediscover the trail of some Far West of my consciousness, leading in some direction in which I could go adventuring, filled with the confusing forces of adolescence. And here was Alejandro Jodorowsky, revealing himself as a dancer of the frontier, a cosmic clown shaped by immemorial wisdom and futuristic imagination.

At first without having approached him in person, what

I admired in him was the multivoiced creator, the Panic-instigator, the burlesque sorcerer, the picaresque character traveling through the shimmering network of traditions, archetypes, and forms of expression, gathering beams of light and mixing them in his cauldron in order to concoct an elixir of awakening, of which we were allowed a few sips, sometimes in the form of a film, sometimes a *bande dessinée,* sometimes a novel, or even a lecture-happening.

I wandered into an art/experimental cinema where, by chance, *El Topo* and *The Holy Mountain* were playing. This Jodorowsky was manifestly not a stunted intellectual, but a heroic figure. I became determined to meet him and gave him a prominent place in the midst of my little personal pantheon.

In matters of human contact, as in all other things, haste is a bad guide; therefore I did not seek to bring about the meeting, convinced that it would occur on its own.

And it did, thirty years later. I should explain that although I had long been aware of the talks given by Jodorowsky in his "Mystic Cabarets," I never thought it suitable for me to attend. The meeting I hoped for was more intimate.

And behold, at the beginning of this year 1989, propitious for so many revolutions, Marc de Smedt asked me to find this man for the magazine *Nouvelles Clés,* in order to pick his brain regarding his interactions in Mexico with Carlos Castaneda, another heroic figure surrounded by his own smoky halo.

Telling myself that these two sorcerers must have had an understanding between them, I picked up the telephone and found myself listening to a melodious voice that told me to come to Vincennes immediately if I wanted a chance to conduct my interview. "You see, I leave tomorrow, I take the airplane at two o'clock in the afternoon . . ."

"Could we not meet in the morning?"

"No, tonight I have my lecture, then I have dinner with my family, and I go to bed at four in the morning. Tomorrow, I sleep until eleven, and I take the airplane. So you must come now."

Understanding that this devil of a man was not one of those people who live riveted to a schedule, and that with him it was best to act on the spur of the moment, I hung up the phone, shoved a blank cassette and tape recorder into a bag, and abandoned the battlefield of my office to catch a taxi for Vincennes, where Jodorowsky lived with his family.

My friend Christian Charrière, founder of the Bureau of Dreams, had taught me to listen for the "confused words" that reality whispers to us, to travel through the world as if it were a "forest of symbols." Thus I noted that my demiurge happened to live on the "Boulevard de la Libération." The taxi driver, understandably, got lost and drove around several streets before dropping me on the aforesaid boulevard, in front of a little garden—a presage of innocence regained.

The house I entered was obviously devoted to creativity: there was a piano at which a very young boy was toiling, a drum set, a typewriter, a great many books, and above all, a vague feeling of freedom, a climate of joyous spontaneity, very far removed from the malaise that one sometimes feels in those homes that are called "bohemian" but are in fact abandoned to sloppiness. At last, the master of the house stood before me, in a vast library, a space consecrated to books and furnished only with two or three chairs. It was as if the thousands of volumes were surrounding emptiness, delimiting a void, in which we now had to fill the space.

This cave of knowledge was accessed by walking through the house and another larger garden at the bottom of which was Jodo's lair. The library windows faced onto vegetation, hence the feeling of open space. To say that Jodorowsky did not disappoint me would be an understatement. Here I risk being relegated to the ranks of the panegyrists. But why? We have descended to the point of not daring to admire anyone, hardened as we are by cynicism.

In these times, when it is customary to dwell upon the limitations of one's fellow humans in order to feel better in one's own mediocrity, I dare to reclaim the right to admire. Not in the manner of those who undiscerningly put someone else on a pedestal, hoping to unload their burdens upon him, and often end up setting fire to the object of their admiration; but rather, in the manner of those who are, if not "strong," sufficiently sure of themselves to doff their hats and thrive on doing so. The former leads to imitation, the latter to elevation. As Emerson wrote, "The young man reveres men of genius, because, to speak truly, they are more himself than he is." I subscribe to these words and truly believe the recognition of the accomplishments of others—whatever may be their necessary imperfections—to be the seeds of my own accomplishment.

Face to face with Jodorowsky, I was immediately struck by his simplicity and touching goodness. I felt welcomed, treated as a familiar, even though I was a stranger by all appearances. (On this subject see the explanations given by Jodo himself over the course of our interviews.)

Alejandro told me of his dazzling encounter with Carlos

Castaneda, the magician of the devil's weed, of the almost vanished race of legend-makers. Once this subject was exhausted, I prepared to leave, but my host, observing me out of the corner of his eye as I got ready, asked me:

"Why are you leaving now? You are in a hurry?"

"Oh, no . . ."

"Then," he persisted gently, "stay, speak with me a little more. . . ." And although I had lost the thread of our conversation, we now resumed it, full of spontaneity and enlightening profundity.

I have been around enough famous people to know that some of them like to make an impression on the young people who come to absorb their words. But with Jodorowsky I found no trace of this desire to gain the upper hand, spiritual or otherwise. I simply felt the heaviness of that weight that indicates inner experience and great human breadth, and I felt his presence to be tinged with a burlesque note—did he not aspire to be the Raymond Devos of mysticism?—as well as a colorful immoderation, with a very Latin-American flavor.

And we separated on the best of terms. On the way out he showed me how my clothing style betrayed my character and autographed a copy of the booklet in which he narrates the initiatory failure that was, for him, the *Dune* project.

A few months passed, my article was published, and we each kept busy in our own way. But I remembered, nostalgically, that melodious accent that is unfortunately lost from Jodorowsky's words once they were printed on paper. It was then that I resolved to devote a volume to him in the collection *À Mots ouverts* [In Open Words].

The temptation was all the stronger because Jodo is one

of those few people who really has something to say: not to join in some sort of journalistic chatter, but to speak the word that illuminates reality. With him, as one can see from reading these interviews, the anecdote is never gratuitous. Often amusing it leads to unsuspected perspectives, like a Zen story. What is extraordinary about Jodorowsky's language is that its field of action is the frontier between the personal and the universal: it reflects his view, which discerns the timeless within the immediate and gauges the everyday by the measure of eternity.

Therefore, I picked up the telephone in order to present my project to its subject. If some personality makes no difficulty about granting a short interview, it is usual—and reasonable—to consider a full-length project, perhaps a book of interviews.

Sensing that my interlocutor was susceptible to disregarding these customs, I placed a cassette in my bag before rushing off to the Boulevard de la Libération. I found Jodo in his garden, armed with a pair of shears, and we headed straightaway for his den.

I was about to start discussing contracts and justifying my plan, but I had hardly had time to sit down when my host said, without any other preamble: "You want to make a book of interviews? *Bueno,* let's begin. Do the interview now. You have a tape?"

"Uh, yes," I stammered, waving around a C-90, "but no tape recorder . . ."

At this point Jodo called one of his sons, who immediately brought us a portable recorder, and I was invited to begin, at a moment's notice, a series of conversations destined for publication, divested of my usual battery of questions and of all preparation save my long-standing familiarity with Jodorowsky's work. There was no question at all of discussing contracts or other concrete matters. Given the ease with which our first interview had come about, I realized that it made no sense to stick to conventional methods. With such a phenomenal personality, I decided that the best method was to have none beyond keeping a guiding thread to our conversations. To our great delight we continued for the next few days in the mode of "Panic" interview-happenings.

These days spent under the sun of Jodo were "Panics," without a doubt. As luck would have it, I was in the middle of a move at the time, a highly symbolic situation in itself. Sometime before we had begun our interviews, burglars had broken into my old apartment and stolen my answering machine and the equipment that I used exclusively for recording my interviews. At the end of our first recorded conversation, Jodo and I went to a neighborhood café where I recounted this misadventure. "It's bizarre," he reflected, "they stole your instruments of communication . . ."

Having finished our drinks we rose and left the café. Upon returning to Alejandro's house, I realized that I had left my bag at the café, containing all my papers, a checkbook, and worst of all, the cassette onto which we had just recorded our conversation. I ran back, but to my despair there was no trace of my precious bag. Seriously rattled, I pondered the meaning of these events: what to think of this new theft, occurring at the moment when Jodo had encouraged me to meditate upon the symbolism of the preceding one?

Jodo, in any case, never stopped talking: there I was, symbolically stripped of my identity (my papers), my possessions (my checkbook), my work, and the knowledge that had been communicated to me (the cassette), and all this while my belongings were in transition from one apartment to the other. I felt as if I were between two homes, between two lives as it were, in a sort of "Bardo," an initiatory limbo . . . not to mention my love life, which, at the time, was pretty well in pieces.

A message was being sent to me: Beware of the scattering of things! Watch out for dispersal! Pull yourself together or stagnate into purgatory . . .

At that moment I decided to do everything I could to recover the stolen cassette. As for Jodo he was completely undisturbed by these vicissitudes and told me: "The next time you come, we continue, until the point where we stop"—some involuntary irony due to the psychomagician's sometimes rough French—"and if you have not found the cassette, then we begin again . . ."

There were many conversations with the North African proprietor of the fateful café, who was thrilled to have discovered in the French newspaper *Libération* (again!) the photo of his filmmaker client. Moustapha—that was his name—finally revealed to me the identity of the thief, a junkie who was a regular at the bar.

I will not recount all the details of our transactions. Suffice it to say that one morning I slipped into the phone booth at the café and rummaged through a garbage bag in which I found my possessions: papers, checkbook, and, oh joy, the C-90 containing the Jodorowskian Word.

That whole week unfurled like a comedic film, of which I was the unhappy yet endearing protagonist, rather like Woody Allen. Rushing back and forth to and from Vincennes to talk with Alejandro, I was faced with a persistent reality: since I had placed a stop payment on my stolen checkbook by telephone, I was unable to access any of my money, even though my confirmation letter had not yet reached my bank's far-off headquarters. I attempted to use my ATM card; before my crazed eyes the gorgon of a machine gobbled it up, just at the time when I needed to acquire furniture, settle with the movers, and pay some thirty-six bills. I had no choice but to borrow large sums of money from my most faithful friends.

I called taxis that never came. I made an appointment with the telephone company, and when they did not arrive at the scheduled time to install my telephone, I learned that they had gone on strike, while in my old apartment, the phone kept ringing into emptiness since the answering machine had been stolen. Jodo told me that the previous week he had left an envelope in a café containing fifteen thousand francs in cash and that eight hours later it had been returned to him intact. He saw this as a good omen for our book.

In short these interviews took place in the midst of a period that was agitated to say the least and which, in retrospect, seems to me like a little initiatory tale.

It was the end of August 1989. The summer was over. One morning I retraced the route to Vincennes to find Jodo busy renovating his house from top to bottom. Was it not curious that our interviews had begun while I was in the middle of moving and were now concluding during a time when my interlocutor was remodeling his entire abode? I, for my part, had gotten my affairs in order and was not about to move any more furniture until the next spring cleaning.

Jodo and I went to the café. I had expected to see our acolyte Moustapha there, but learned that he had left—as if to indicate to me that everything in this world passes by—and the café, now run by an older couple, had a more respectable appearance.

Seated in a sunny spot we started to chat, and the magic began working. We talked without any goal, without a tape recorder, but Alejandro's words were to become just as much a part of this book as any others. Once again he had nonchalantly transported me into a world replete with signs and symbols, in which the least incident is a path to explore and in which wonder is the watchword.

We took a few photos ("I should have taken a bath; I look like the Yeti"), then returned to the cavernous library at the bottom of the garden, where Jodo, before my eyes and all in one go, wrote the postscript to this book. Then—after confiding in me his joy at having had lunch in Los Angeles with Stan Lee, the brilliant creator of Spiderman and the Silver Surfer, the first superheroes to be beset by emotional problems—he returned to working on his house. My girlfriend and I went to hang around the flea market in search of utensils necessary for the accomplishment of a psychomagical act suggested by Jodo, regarding the details of which, dear reader, I will remain silent . . .

Now, for you who are presently skimming through these pages, it is time to carry out a little psychomagical act: Tonight, in bed, before you fall asleep, inoculate yourself with this book. Let the Jodorowskian word act upon you during that fertile interval of the night, and awaken in the morning in a fuller and freer place in yourself. Let yourself be touched by this lesson of humanity.

GILLES FARCET
AUGUST 1989

TWO

DIALOGUE—1989
The First Interview

Alejandro, you seem to me such an extraordinary person, one of those characters who are found in adventure stories or initiatory tales. You are a filmmaker, a theater person, a master of the tarot, a storyline writer for bandes dessinées, a novelist, but you escape all these labels to travel further, into a space where the fantastic pervades the everyday. . . . If I am not mistaken, you are sixty years old today?

Sixty years exactly!

At sixty years of age, Alejandro Jodorowsky, who are you?

Bueno . . . . That question is both very simple and very complicated. In general one regards oneself in a set manner, from a fixed point at which one has decided to stay. But one may look at oneself in, so to speak, a prehistoric manner, trying to see who one was before birth. . . . One may judge oneself from the point of view of a dinosaur, a river, a tree, or the magma that one once was. One may judge oneself from the point of view of the creator. One may also consider what one will be after death. . . . One may see oneself as at a thousand years old, ten thousand years, thirty thousand years. . . . One may see oneself with the characteristics of an eternal being. As for me, I see myself as an eternal being. It is something that I have learned to do. I have surpassed death, and I see myself as the collective being that I will be, belonging to universal life. That is how I judge myself, which comes down to saying that I do not judge myself! I love myself! I have a great love for myself. Not a narcissistic love: I have a great love for myself as a divine being. I feel continually amazed when looking at this life that I am, in the present moment, here and now. I am amazed by this splendid illusion, this incredible game. Therefore, in fact, I have no age. . . . But I do not have any name either: that is the truth. In fact, I am not a human being, but a particle, a fragment of totality. You understand this is a question of point of view. Everything depends on where I place myself. You tell me I am sixty years old, but *who* is sixty years old? The universe is not sixty years old; it is millions of years old. My age can be an instant or sometimes a million years. I speak sincerely. I know that all this may appear as a sort of madness, but when one works on oneself, when one pushes back one's mental limits, one ends up feeling these things. Of course, there is a clown in me: This clown is sixty years old, and his existence effectively began in 1929. He is a poet, an acrobat of life. I love him very much and feel a great deal of compassion for him. I also feel compassion for my body. I feel like a prince dressed as a toad. I see my teeth fall out with the same melancholy that seizes me when I see dead leaves in an Indian summer in Canada. I see myself get wrinkles and grow fat. It is a phenomenon that I watch happening as if I were looking at a landscape. I believe that I will view my death in the same fashion, as a marvelous natural phenomenon. It is marvelous to be incarnated as a human! It is also a great joke, something very comical. The worst dramas are comic. . . . In any case, when one feels oneself to be a divine creation, one can only be good.

By this logic we are all divine creations; but we are far from all feeling good! How is it that you, Alejandro, enjoy this privilege?

I have worked a great deal for it, you understand! I have done nothing else. . . . This work began practically with my birth. I am a good child of immigrants, born in northern Chile. . . . I was good, that is a fact; I had that quality, accompanied by a desire to achieve spiritual crystallization.

You experienced this very early on, from early childhood?

Yes, very early . . . I can see myself now at the age of six or seven, sitting before the door to my father's shop, where he sold women's underwear. I was eating a banana. A poor child ran by and snatched the fruit from my hand. I did not weep, but felt pity for this child. And the next day I sat out there again with a banana, waiting for him to steal it from me. So my driving force was goodness, right away. At the same time I have asked myself all the usual questions: Why must I die? Does God exist? When I was eighteen the awareness of my mortal nature struck me like a hammer on the head. I had never properly realized it before then. And I went running through the streets, crying out that I did not want to die! From this moment on I have needed to appease my dread.

Did you have a religious education?

Not at all, or rather, yes: I was raised with the religion of atheism. My father was a fanatical nonbeliever, opposed to any spiritual conception of existence. So that is where I started from. I had to fill this void and explore my being. So I disguised myself like a clown, pursued different trades as if each time I was putting on a new costume: I disguised myself as a puppeteer, a music-hall comedian, a theater and film director, a poet, a novelist, a *bande-dessinée* author, an artist, whatever!

Were you immediately drawn to the artistic dimension of existence?

Yes, to theater and literature. I went to university like any old idiot, but I was disgusted with it. Then my artistic life began, and my family life was added to it. My family has been like a school for me, a work of self-knowledge. And it took about half a century for me to feel truly good. Before that I was always searching, wandering through all the cultures, coming in contact with masters. . . . When I was forty I began to find myself, and at fifty it seemed to me that I had made some real gains.

Let's talk a little more about your schooling. Your spiritual education went hand in hand with your artistic apprenticeship.

Yes, my first masters were five great Chilean poets who shaped my artistic spirit. I was lucky to be born in Chile. Before all the political catastrophes, it was a country of poets, a magical land, like an island. We were contained between the mountain range of the Andes and the Pacific Ocean, in a very surrealist atmosphere of collective madness. In the afternoon when work was over, the Chileans would get drunk, and life became a party. We bathed in a climate of chaos and total euphoria.

At what age did you leave Chile?

I was twenty-three.

What did you do there up until your departure?

First I was devoted to writing, and I endeavored to meet poets who have refined my artistic spirit. With them I learned to return to my own beauty, which is in fact what we all carry within ourselves. Then, in the university environment, I played at being a circus clown. It is hard to convey the ambience of that time there: the philosophy professors didn't hesitate to disguise themselves as clowns, too, rolling around on the ground in front of their students. . . . The sexual revolution took place in Chile long before it spread over the rest of the world. . . . It was a permanent party. Then, after quitting the university, I gave my life over to puppets. I founded my own theater, which was combined with a twenty-four-person university choir. The government loaned us a warship in which we went all around the north of Chile. We toured the mining companies: the choir sang; then I put on my show for the workers and the children.

What were the themes of the shows?

I was inspired by the writings of García Lorca, or else I made up stories that were already very symbolic. I remember one story about a woman who fell in love with a man whose head was a mirror: in other words she fell in love with her own reflection! I also imagined staging a minotaur-Christ, with Socrates and Plato clowns as the choir.

Did you continue to be a puppeteer until you were twenty-three?

No, because after three years devoted to puppets, I discovered the importance of human actors. I realized that the quality of an actor has less to do with what he says than with the sentiment he conveys. So I started doing mute theater, pantomime, and started a troupe, which, by the way, still exists today. I became fairly famous in Chile at the time, leading that company of forty people. We traveled the country . . . I played this role until a decisive crisis took place in me. At a certain moment I saw that I had explored all the possibilities that were offered to me in this country and that in order to advance, I must leave. I had reached a plateau and could no longer learn very much.

You were very young when you achieved what many people strive for all their lives: you began living well off your art; you secured your place.

Yes, I was well known, as I said. I had practically made my own life. I was engaged; it remained only for me to be married, to have children, and to play off my reputation. But this seemed like a dead end to me. One day I suddenly announced to my company that I was departing, leaving everything to them: I owned a big studio, scenery, costumes. I abandoned all these possessions, to the great horror of most of them. I threw my address book into the sea, destroyed all my photos. . . . This is why, today, I do not have any picture of myself as a child or adolescent. I wanted nothing to remain. I never saw my father, my mother, or my friends again. . . . In fact, it is only recently that I rediscovered my father, who is eighty-eight years old. At the time I cut all ties and left without looking back.

Your story makes me think of the sannyasins, those Hindu renunciates who burned their identity papers and clothes, severed all family ties, and gave themselves over to wandering.

Yes, this was truly a way of ending life in order to be reborn.

This goes far beyond the feeling of professional stagnation; you went through a sort of "death to yourself" of a mystical order.

Exactly. I was driven to distraction by not finding divinity, by not discovering cosmic love in myself.

You knew that this divinity existed?

I wanted it to exist! On the one hand I did not believe in it, because of my upbringing. I thought that I would never arrive at faith. On the other hand I hoped desperately to encounter the divine. I lived in constant fear of death, all my being was revolted at the prospect of my demise. I searched for an answer but did not find it. I should mention that during that epoch, at the beginning of the 1950s, I knew nothing at all of oriental mysticism, of Zen.

Did you know that the Hindu mystic Ramana Maharshi achieved enlightenment after feeling terrible fear while thinking of death?

Ah, yes! I remember my first great attack of fear of death,

after a marvelous night of partying in Chile. I must have been nineteen years old. Our house had burned; only my room had been spared! So my friends and I had a huge party there, a celebration of burning. I wore a coat of flames, disguised as fire. Around three or four in the morning, everyone was drunk, and we ended up at the market, eating cheese. I was swimming in happiness. And all at once I realized that all my friends would die, that the whole city would die, that the Earth would die, that the stars would die . . . that nothing would be spared, least of all me. It was a sort of negative enlightenment. Suddenly sober I saw how the city was bathed in anguish, how the people around me were prey to this fear, unable to face it. From that day on I had to come into contact with divinity in order to appease my terror.

You did not yet know about Zen or Hinduism; weren't you tempted by Catholicism?

No, my father had influenced me too much. He was a Jew who renounced everything. I had watched him throw crosses, stars of David, and statuettes of the Virgin down the toilet, repeating in an obsessive manner: "This does not exist, this does not exist. . . ." He spat in front of synagogues and insulted the priests he met on the street. He told me over and over: "After death there is nothing, you rot, that is all." In short I had never been prepared to accept a religious vision of things. That said—my friends and I, being poets—played around a good deal with the Bible and the Gospels. We grasped them above all through Dostoevsky's *Idiot,* and so this was more of a literary game. I had also been surprised by the case of a young man who, after working intensely on puppets with me for fifteen days, decided to become a Benedictine monk. I had been rather harsh with him because I found him stupid, and now, suddenly, he was announcing to me that he was going into a monastery and thanking me for what I'd done for him! I protested: "I've found nothing in my life, and you're thanking me!" He answered: "You'll understand one day." This was my only direct contact with a true Christian.

You left Chile voluntarily for France. Why France?

Because it was the country of Marcel Marceau, and I wanted to work with him. I went to see him perform, and I had the idea of offering him my criticisms. I was naive; I did not know how things work in the cultural world. In my country success had come to me without my making the least effort. So I made notes, numbered from one to seven, writing my observations on the program. . . . Then I went to give it all to him. He was furious. "By what right are you giving me these notes? Who are you to judge my work? Go away and never come back!" I left, very surprised and a little ashamed of my tactlessness, while also telling myself that I was not obliged to appreciate his show indiscriminately. Finally I went to find him at his school and told him: "Listen, mime is my life. You must give me a test to see if I am capable of working for you." He agreed to see me perform and immediately hired me for his company. That is how I went from the status of troupe director to being a minor actor.

At the same time I began a spiritual quest after realizing that the art of mime is generally saturated with anguish and malaise. A euphoric—or even just joyous—dimension was lacking. And I understood that the sadness of mimes came from the fact that they did not integrate the sacred dimension of their art into their movements. They confined themselves to being sad clowns. Now, a mime works with his body! Is there any material more sacred than the human body? So I began to question my vocation. I had become one of Marceau's partners. This was not anything too great: it consisted of holding his placards and doing one or two individual pantomimes in which one had to stick to technique and not express any emotion. But in fact this was the highest level one could rise to in his company.

How long did you spend with him?

Five years. This allowed me to travel the world on his tours. Then one day he had the idea of developing his troupe further. He envisaged giving me great roles, but then I announced my departure. Everyone was devastated. I got along well with Marceau, and he tried to reason with me: "You are crazy to leave now, at the moment when you could have finally had your proper place. Why are you leaving?" I answered that I had to go because I no longer believed in what I was doing. He had trouble understanding my thought process: "You will fall into poverty," he told me; "That doesn't matter. I will be poor." I shook hands with everyone and left. Marceau wept and so did I, and we embraced. But I had to break from that structure, which no longer fit me spiritually.

It seems there is a recurring pattern in your life: you follow a certain path until you reach success or the concrete possibility of success; then at the moment when you could enjoy your gains and settle down, you bow out for fear of succumbing to spiritual and professional rigidity.

Oh yes, this has happened to me plenty of times! Much later, after having made my film *El Topo,* which was a great success in the United States, I was offered a great deal of money to make a film of *The Story of O.* All the newspapers wanted to interview me; I was going to be on the cover of *Playboy, Penthouse.* . . . The journalists could already see their headlines: "Avant-Garde Director Films *Story of O*". . . . Fifteen minutes after signing the contract, I escaped, though I had two hundred thousand dollars practically in my hand. I refused the money and left for other adventures.

Let us return to mime: you stayed in contact with Marceau?

Certainly! I wrote pantomimes for him with the idea that through Marceau, I could create something that would go beyond the level of clown and touch the sacred dimension. When one truly loves something or someone, one cannot abandon it. So I had to offer a little of my creativity to the art of mime.

What did you do after leaving Marceau?

I became a house painter, moonlighting of course. But it was also a form of initiation. There were three of us working together: one was a disciple of Gurdjieff, and the other, an Arab, was observing Ramadan.

Your existence seems perpetually full of "chances" that could qualify as "objective," to use the surrealist term.

You know, around the same time, walking in Paris, I passed a trash can in which there was a cheetah's tail. I glued it to my rear then went to a costume party near the Opera. It was at this party that I met surrealists to whom I became profoundly connected and who introduced me to [André] Breton.

Moving among these circles, I suppose that despite every-thing you hardly can have wanted to remain a house painter.

I had to earn a living! But at the same time, I continued to work on the stage. I did a music-hall number with some singers called "The Three Horaces" who were somewhat successful at the time. I showed them a mime that they integrated into their show. Then one day Maurice Chevalier came to find me, in a car, which had, fittingly, cheetah-skin seats.

Maurice Chevalier? Why you?

He had seen me with The Three Horaces and wanted me to help him put on a show that was meant to revive his career. So I worked with him. During this period I got near many famous singers. . . . But what was important was my inner search, which I was continuing for better or worse.

You still had no master?

The others were my masters! In each person who crossed my path, I sought an upaguru, an auxiliary master, as they are called in India. Every encounter might turn out to hold rich lessons: a woman who ran a little esoteric bookshop showed me the Marseilles tarot; a friend who had come from Chile knocked on my door one day at three o'clock in the afternoon, while I was sleeping. He insulted me, saying that instead of sleeping so late, I ought to practice judo, and he took me to a dojo! It is thanks to him that I now understand the impor-tance of the martial arts. So I can say that in this regard, he was an unforgettable master for me.

I've been told that you became quite good at karate.

There was a time when I practiced a lot. But in the end I gave it up, because I had no desire to fight. In my whole life I have never hit anyone.

So you spent several years in France, during which you basically had encounters, dabbled in various aspects of musical theater, and filled the gaps in your budget by becoming a house painter. How did this period come to an end?

One day Marceau announced to me that he was leaving for Mexico. He needed someone, and he asked me to help him out. I agreed, went there, and ended up staying. I earned my living as a professor of pantomime, then as a theater director. My career was punctuated by scandals, insofar as I truly contributed to establishing avant-garde theater in Mexico. I put on about a hundred plays, choosing from playwrights such as Ionesco, Adamov, Strindberg, Beckett. . . . It was a time of professional effervescence. But since we are talking about spiritual masters, I must mention that it was in Mexico that I met a Zen roshi from whom I learned an enormous amount. Before meeting him I had never before been around a true mystic. His name was Ejo Takata.

How did you meet him, under what circumstances?

I went looking for him. You see, at the time in Mexico there was a psychoanalyst named Erich Fromm. He lived in Cuernavaca and had founded a group, a school of psychoanalysis. Fromm himself, as I knew him, was a very gentle being, very human, very transparent. His disciples, by contrast, were ill at ease, and

Fromm asked me to teach them a course in bodily expression so that they could stop moving like toads! So I hung around Fromm and his school for a year, and we eventually talked about Zen. D. T. Suzuki had come to give lectures in Mexico and had made a profound mark. Fromm himself was very impressed. These conversations reminded me of everything I had seen in Japan when I was there on tour with Marceau. I had visited Zen temples without understanding anything, such a Western barbarian, and yet something had touched me deeply. Then I learned that Fromm knew a Japanese Zen master. A group of doctors were staying in a little house, the address of which was kept secret. I ended up bribing a member of the group to reveal the location to me, and I immediately presented myself before the master.

Did you quickly become close to him?

Actually one day the master realized that all these doctors who were monopolizing him were not playing by the rules of meditation. They were taking pills, undoubtedly LSD, and not following his instructions. Furious, Ejo Takata sent them all packing and consequently found himself without lodging and without disciples. At the time I was living in a little house that cost me next to nothing, and I proposed to the master that he come to give his teachings at my place.

What was his manner of teaching? How did he work with you?

The first time I went to see him, before he moved in with me, I knocked on the door and found myself face to face with an ageless Japanese man who smiled at me. He received me as if

I were one of his old friends and showed me an ideogram. I asked him what its meaning was, and he answered: *"Felicidad,"* "Happiness." This was the first lesson. For the second lesson he told me: "Come meditate." He brought out two wooden stools, and we sat to meditate. Then he said to me: "Now, when you come back, you bring your stool." That was the second lesson. . . . We got straight to the heart of things, considering that he spoke almost no Spanish, save two or three words. I had to learn by watching him; he taught by example. His manner was very different from that of Deshimaru. This latter was a great master, but he addressed the European mind and had adapted his teaching as a consequence. But most of the time, with the exception of the doctors I just mentioned, Ejo Takata talked to Indians, Mexican natives. His lessons were very tough; he hit us very hard with his stick.

So you worked with him for five years?

Yes, until he was gone.

What do you mean? Did he die?

No, one day he vanished. It was as if he dissolved into nature. . . . It is a real legend in Mexico today.

Why did he leave?

He suddenly realized that it was no use to meditate with a little group of intellectuals or to have a favorite disciple when there was hunger in Mexico. So he started traveling around Mexico to teach the Indians how to grow soybeans. He was hunted, some people wanted to kill him, considering him a communist. . . . And so he led a sort of war, which he won, because today all of Mexico produces soybeans. No one knows it, but Ejo Takata, wherever he may be now, is present in all the grocery stores in Mexico. What a lesson for me, to see him leave in order to fill the stomachs of the Indians, to vanish into the landscape!

Did you feel abandoned when he left?

To tell the truth I did not want to consider myself as his student. I envisaged our relationship more as a friendship. . . . In fact, I lacked love. I was terrified of becoming a disciple. And yet I was well and truly a disciple, without knowing it. Today, several decades later, I can love him and thank him. You see for a long time I was lacking in faith, in generosity. To compensate I imitated nonviolent behavior. At my core I was not peaceful at all: I could have beaten up an army of people! But I understood the importance of this nonviolent attitude, so I forced myself to have it.

Is it good to force oneself in this manner?

For me it was good. I had no faith, while knowing at the same time that faith was the only solution. So I trusted in God. I imitated the attitude of a believer full of faith, even though I did not believe. And these attitudes ended up becoming integrated into my nature.

To take all the risks with which your life has been punctuated, you must have had confidence in Providence.

Today, I see Providence at work everywhere. There is something magical in my existence. I have the feeling of having always been miraculously spared.

So Ejo Takata left you, but you also encountered an extraordinary woman in Mexico, the sorceress, Pachita.

Yes, one day a friend took me to see this old woman who healed people. There I witnessed unexplainable phenomena that still surprises me and leaves me perplexed today. I never said "this is real," nor did I ever say "this is fake." I cannot deliver a verdict regarding the nature of the miracles that took place before my eyes.

What miracles? Can you give me some examples?

I saw people, many of them French, operated upon. This was done in a rather brutal manner. Pachita operated with a knife and a pair of scissors. I even saw her transplant a heart. . . . I can tell you about the case of the wife of the French film director François Reichenbach, who had a great deal of spine trouble after an accident. Pachita healed her successfully.

How did she proceed?

She went into trances. She often asked me to read poems to her that made her fall into a trance. Then she operated. It was a hard spectacle to watch. The room stank of blood, excrement; people vomited.

Was this reality or a perfect illusion?

I don't know what to say. She worked by the light of one candle; consequently we were plunged into semidarkness. For a while I thought she was performing a conjuring trick.

Were the sick people healed?

Some were. Those who believed were healed.

Is it true that you yourself resorted to using her services?

Yes, I had pain in my liver, and I was curious to experience an operation on myself. Pachita told me that I had a liver tumor and agreed to heal me. I played along with it, telling myself that she couldn't kill me. In fact, she had already operated on so many people that she would have been imprisoned long ago if she had harmed any of her patients.

Weren't you afraid of suffering, of pain?

No, because for me, this was theater. I wanted to go through it and see what it was like; that is why I did it. That said, I started to be afraid once I was stretched out on the bed with Pachita in front of me, armed with a big knife and surrounded by the praying faithful. I wanted to get out, but it was too late. I thought she was going to chop me up with her scissors.

Did you feel pain?

Yes, I felt as much pain as anyone whose flesh is cut with scissors! The blood flowed, and I told myself I was going to die. Then she cut me in the belly with her knife, and I felt as if my bowels were being opened.

That must have been horrible.

It was terrible! Never in my life have I felt such pain. I suffered dreadfully for about eight minutes and turned white as a sheet. Pachita made me an infusion, and little by little I felt the blood flow back into my body. Then it was as if she tore my liver out. Finally she passed her hands over my belly to close the wound, and instantly the pain was gone! If this was conjuring, the illusion was perfect: not only did the people present see the blood flow and the abdomen opened up, but also the patient himself felt the pain! After that I was healed and never had any more liver trouble. Beyond just getting healed this was one of the great experiences of my life. This woman was a mountain, as impressive as a mythical Tibetan Lama. I have never felt such panicked fear and never felt so much gratitude as when she announced to me that I was healed and could go. In that moment I saw in her the universal Mother. What a psychological shock! Pachita was a great psychologist; she knew the human soul. It matters little whether these operations were real or fake: the results were there. With regard to magic I am not so concerned with the authenticity or illusory character of the phenomenon. What interests me is the outcome. Pachita was well intentioned. Whether she was a true magician or a brilliant conjuror, she did not heal people for the money.

I would love it if you could clarify what you gained from this encounter with Pachita, the depth of what you drew from it.

She gave me the understanding and the experience of a nonintellectual person-to-person contact. As soon as Pachita touched you, it was as if you were a child again. She knew the true language of the body.

I can also say that she taught me magic. Quite simply she initiated me to what I call psychomagic today. Like poetry magic is an action that works upon reality and transforms it. Normally actions are merely the results of forces at work in reality. In magic the action is an agent, a creative force.

Do you mean that instead of being part of cause-effect chains, magic acts upon the chains themselves?

And breaks them!

Are you a magician yourself?

A psychomagician, perhaps. . . . Some people reproach me for speaking in this way; but today we live in a world where one is barely allowed to speak well of oneself. One can't speak about one's own merit without being judged as a megalomaniac or fanatic. Truly people refuse to respect themselves. But in my case I have no desire to talk about my failures. I would rather talk about my successes, insofar as they can serve as an example and be helpful to certain people who find themselves inspired by them. That is the spirit in which I am saying all this. Therefore, today, I consider myself adept at helping those who come to me, because my subconscious is no longer my enemy. I have not had any nightmares for a long time. So I am somewhat like a computer. If you ask a precise question, the computer answers, and that's all! I give automatic responses that spring up directly from the depths. From my contact with Pachita and other sages, I learned to address myself to a person while perceiving the suffering child within him. This is my psychomagic.

It was also in Mexico, and during the same time period, that you met Carlos Castaneda. Castaneda is an elusive character whom few people can even boast of having seen. Under what circumstances did you meet him?

At this time, in the 1970s, I was very famous in certain circles thanks to my film *El Topo*, which for many people was a sort of field guide to initiatory cinema. Castaneda had seen

El Topo twice and had really loved it. I was at a restaurant in Mexico that serves big steaks and good wine. I was there with a Mexican actress, who spotted one of her friends sitting at another table with a gentleman. Castaneda—for that was the gentleman—learned who I was and sent her over to my table. She asked me if I wanted to meet Castaneda. "Certainly," I answered, "I admire him greatly!" She suggested that he come to sit with me, but I got up myself and went over to his table.

That's a coincidence worthy of a novel.

Life is like a novel! I suggested to Castaneda that I could go to visit him, but he wanted to come to my hotel. We were like two Chinese people competing at politeness. He kept putting himself down to exalt me, and I did the same with him.

Did you ever doubt that you were truly in the presence of Castaneda?

No, not for a moment. Later, in the United States, a book came out in which there was a picture of him, a drawing. It is the portrait of the man I met.

What was your first impression?

In Mexico it is very easy to tell what social class someone belongs to, simply from his physique. Castaneda had the physique of a busboy.

Yes, he looked plebeian, not tall but stocky, with curly hair, the nose a bit flattened, one might say a Mexican born into the working class. But as soon as he spoke, he was transformed into a prince; one could sense great learning behind every one of his words.

Did he give you an impression of wisdom?

Not wisdom, but sympathy. We felt like friends immediately. He was simply dressed and was eating a big steak washed down with Beaujolais. . . . He was not like Don Juan, but like the Castaneda who is expressed in the books. I could hear that tone, that voice, so to speak.

In your view do his books recount true facts, or are they fiction?

It is difficult for me to judge. My impression is that they are based on true experiences, from which he extrapolates; he introduces concepts drawn from universal initiatory literature. In his books one finds Zen, the Upanishads, the Tarot, work on dreams. . . . One thing is certain: he definitely traveled around Mexico to do his research.

Do you believe in the existence of Don Juan?

No, I believe that this person is a brilliant invention by Castaneda, who actually met several Yaqui sorcerers.

How did your final conversation go in the hotel?

First he called to tell me he was coming five minutes early! I was touched by this gesture, so thoughtful. Then he arrived, and I said: "I do not know if you are a madman, a genius, a conman, or if you speak the truth." He assured me that he spoke nothing but the truth and set about telling me an incredible story, explaining how Don Juan, with a simple tap on the back, sent him forty kilometers away—because Castaneda let himself be distracted by a passing woman. . . . He also told me about the sex life of Don Juan, who was capable of ejaculating fifteen times in a row. It seemed to me that Castaneda himself liked women a lot. He asked me if we could make a film together. Hollywood had offered him a lot of money, but he did not want Don Juan to be played by Anthony Quinn. . . . Then he began to have diarrhea. He started having great pains in his stomach, which he told me never happened to him normally, and I myself felt violent pain in my liver and right leg! It was strange to feel these pains just when we were beginning to envisage a project. . . . We lay around the room. I called a taxi for him, and sent him back to his hotel. Then I went to have Pachita operate on me. I had suggested that Castaneda come to meet that incredible woman, but he didn't show up. Then I was bedridden for three days. Once I was up and around again, I called his hotel, but he was gone. I never saw him again; life separated us. A warrior leaves no traces.

So he seemed to you to be both a trickster and someone very interesting at the same time.

He told me his stories about Don Juan with such conviction . . . I am used to theater, to actors, and I never had the feeling that he was lying. Perhaps he is a mad genius?

In your opinion what is Castaneda's contribution?

His contribution is immense: He has created a different source of knowledge, the South American source. He has revived the concept of the spiritual warrior. . . . He has brought to light the idea of working on lucid dreams. Without a doubt he published too much, but the American publishers had him sign contracts for about ten books. . . . And always, despite everything, he has something new to say. His books reveal many forgotten things. So, true or false, it doesn't matter. If it's trickery, then it is sacred trickery.

Let's linger on this idea of "sacred trickery." From this perspective the purity of intention and the power of the symbol at work count for more than the notions of "true" and "false."

Absolutely! Up to age fifty I did a lot of good for a great number of people while *imitating* generosity. They are still thanking me today! At that time it was nothing but pure imitation on my part; but I was well intentioned. So what does it matter? The work is what's important.

During those years in Mexico, you often returned to France, and it was during this period that you made cultural history by founding the "Panic" movement with the playwright Arrabal and the artist Topor.

That happened before my encounter with Ejo Takata. Because, I should explain, my encounter with Zen modified my way of seeing and my behavior. Topor is an atheist; Arrabal fairly recently converted to Catholicism. . . . But at the time we were young, and we wanted to go beyond the surrealism that depended too much on Breton's taste. Certainly he had perfect taste; he was a refined man, a gentleman of exquisite politeness. But we wanted to surpass surrealism. We wanted to mock what is known as culture. Therefore we tried to create a movement that had not yet existed. This, again, was "sacred trickery." In fact, this movement never really came into existence. However, I am going back to Spain again soon to join Arrabal for a television broadcast about "Panic."

Despite all that you organized events under this label.

Yes, we put on "happenings."

Which, it seems, were very violent.

Extremely violent!

Why? I don't suppose this was a matter of a simple release of tension.

You see, whenever I do art, I begin with violence. Why? Because this world is violent, and one finds peace by traversing violence. In my film *El Topo,* as in the happenings, I sacrificed several animals because I believed that death had to be present as a driving force for enlightenment. I could not sacrifice a human being, and so I wanted the animals to be immolated, as in the Old Testament. These animals, in my mind, were participating in a ritual. Today I don't do it anymore, but at that time I was on a search, and it seemed to me to be justified.

I read that you cut the throats of chickens on stage.

One or two. For me it was like cutting my own head off. I had to pass through violence and crime. Like Breton I believe that "Beauty will be convulsive or will not be at all."*

The great mistake made by some spiritual groups who seek to produce art is that they make it into some little thing that is sappy or naive . . . or too folkloric. All such sentimentality has no resemblance to authentic art. A real artist who has no mystical quest or training can still inflict a great shock, a profound revelation, if his expression is true. Conversely, a guru does not

*[The quote is from the final page of Breton's book *Nadja* (1928). —*Trans.*]

necessarily have to be a great artist. I do not understand why emasculated art is produced in the name of spiritual peace. The violent forces of nature must be integrated and channeled.

Which is what you did in your films. How did you get into filmmaking?

Bueno, as I've told you, I did a lot of theater in Mexico. But film was what I always wanted to do. It combined all my various talents. I knew how to draw, make costumes, sets, music, direct, write plays. . . . In film I saw the art par excellence of our epoch, which would allow me to make the best use of my accumulated experience. What's more, theater is a cry that resounds throughout the city, but the cry of film is heard round the world.

Was it bothering you that unlike film recorded on reels, theater is a fleeting creation that vanishes after each performance?

Yes, because I wanted to touch the whole world, to deliver a more universal message. Remember, I had been the instigator of the happening, the "mayfly of panic." Theater is a phenomenon that dissolves into nothingness; one cannot view the exact same performance every night. Conclusion: It is no use trying to vanquish time in striving to make things stay the same. It is better just to play upon the ephemeral, to use the elements that die in the very moment they are used: smoke, animals, vegetables, things that are broken. . . . The event can only happen once. At this time I had a fair amount of money thanks to pantomimes such as "The Cage" or "The Maskmaker" that I had written with Marceau. Marceau was at the height of his fame, and the royalties were rolling in. I was asked to participate in a festival of free expression in France, and I decided to use all my money to create a gigantic happening. The organizer was very surprised, even upset, because the creators of "happenings" were generally devoid of means. For this spectacle I collaborated with a very rich and very artistic young man, Yves Leyaouanc. I always walked around with a huge amount of money in my pockets; he pulled out an enormous wad of cash in front of me. We put the two piles of money together on a table and combined them, giving birth to a spectacle of incredible luxury. There were great mirrors in the room that we broke, a reproduction of Rodin's *Thinker,* and a Volkswagen.

I suppose one doesn't leave such an event unscathed.

For me this happening marked the death of my theatrical career; in a six-hour spectacle, I satisfied all my ambitions and fantasies in the role of stage director. It was a stripping down, a putting to death of the theater man I had been. I had my head shaved, and at the end I found myself in such a state of purity that the birds released during the performance landed on me and stayed there. After this happening I wanted to break away from the past, to shatter a certain narcissistic image I had of myself. And I succeeded; my narcissism was literally exploded. During the course of this spectacle, I had myself whipped, I lost a front tooth, and I almost killed myself by falling with an iron apparatus around my neck. That's when a paranormal phenomenon took place: I saw myself falling and I said to myself, "This is the end; I'm going to break my neck." Suddenly time stopped, I watched my fall in slow motion, and I was able to control it perfectly, so that I did not lose my life, but only one tooth! Generally speaking I have observed that time stops when one is in great danger.

So this unusual happening was like a new death for you, and a rebirth.

All the more so because the organizer, Jean-Jacques Lebel, was so furious that he did everything he could do to make this event vanish into total oblivion. There was not a single article, not even a gossip column! This was an enormous lesson for me. I gave everything, to the point that I left the event sick and had to stay in bed, exhausted by the effort. It was my most beautiful achievement, and the ill will of one single person was enough to reduce it to nothing! A bit later, six months after, *Planète* described it as the greatest happening ever put on, but at the time, nothing. . . . Even the two hours of film shot during the spectacle have disappeared. A great silence has fallen upon this work. In short it was like a failed triumph. This was very good for me. My theatrical personality was literally immolated in an extravagant ritual sacrifice. There was a succession of strange circumstances. For example, Topor and Arrabal were meant to participate. Four hours before the start of the spectacle, they sent me a prostitute who announced that they were not coming. I had to replace them on the spur of the moment. The next day, at the Comédie Française, they threw themselves at my feet excusing themselves, saying that they were faithless men. We had a good laugh, and our friendship did not suffer, but all the same it was curious.

In fact, the temporary weaknesses and doubts of others only make us stronger.

Once dead to theater you jumped into the adventure of film.

I began by filming Arrabal's piece, *Fando and Lis,* in Mexico.

That project took place under very particular conditions. There was a syndicate there without whose authorization one could not shoot films. The managers of this syndicate were people who talked about film constantly, but rarely shot anything. Buñuel was their god. I like Buñuel a lot, but I wanted to reveal myself as an iconoclast. One day I went to a cocktail party that the syndicate was hosting in honor of the great filmmaker. They were all there, seated, fawning over their idol. All of a sudden I approached him and spoke with him familiarly, and he did the same, to the great outrage of the others. Then I observed that Buñuel's trousers had an oval pocket that looked a lot like a woman's genitals. While the people were discussing film, I amused myself by putting my hand right into this vaginal pocket of Buñuel's and moving it around, as if I were raping him. The others were furious to see me being so disrespectful! Then I defied them, saying: "You are cowards, impotent intellectuals. You talk about film without acting on it. I will show you what can be accomplished. I will film when I want to, despite the syndicate, despite the police, despite everyone, at my will. I will bypass you. Even worse, I will begin next month!" Then, without permission, I gradually gathered the funds (only thirty thousand dollars) for shooting in black and white on Saturdays and Sundays. Once the film was finished, I showed it to an important person who was intelligent enough to understand my process. He put *Fando and Lis* on the program for the Acapulco film festival. The scandal caused by my defiance of the syndicate proved to be so enormous that the festival could not weather it and never took place again! But afterward the syndicates opened up to young directors, and things changed. That is how I began my cinematographic career.

Fando and Lis *is a very symbolic piece, in an initiatory sense. Did you want to make an initiatory film from the start?*

Right from the start.

What exactly do you understand "initiatory film" to mean?

A film in which one makes one's way toward a more and more acute realization. For me initiation is nothing more than becoming more conscious. Conscious of what? Of everything. A conscious being is a connected being. All my films are simply a search for consciousness. My cinematic debut coincided with my meeting with Ejo Takata, whose mark is very present in my second film *El Topo.*

What was your inspiration for El Topo?

You know, it's very difficult for an artist to talk about his inspiration. Being an artist doesn't mean being good or bad, having or not having talent; it means feeling an absolute and total need to create, to the point where one cannot *not* create. For me, at the time, making films was an imperative need. After making *El Topo* and *Holy Mountain,* I made no more films for fifteen years, not because I couldn't anymore, but because I had nothing to say. An alchemical process had to take place in my being in order for me to feel any new desire to make a film. That is why, at this present time, I have just finished making *Santa Sangre.*

We've been talking about violence in art; El Topo *is an extremely brutal film. And it's a work of art! Someone recently told me that* Santa Sangre *was "delirious."*

For me remarks of this sort totally displace the problem. I come from the avant-garde school, and when I look at a work, I am not preoccupied with knowing whether it is "violent," "delirious," or whatever. . . . I only ask myself: Is it a strong creation, a living creation? I know people full of good intentions, full of idealism, who write peaceful music, little insipid melodies that are supposed to bring peace and good vibrations. Their intentions are laudable, but with their rose-colored music, they can't hold a candle to the least skilled rock musician! Picasso's *Guernica* is a painting of extreme violence; artistically it is a marvel. Every artistic act possesses a monumental force that can potentially endure through the ages.

In any case art brings into play all the forces that are present in the universe. Nature is not sugar-coated.

Nature is very violent! I have sometimes heard of certain gurus who take pride in doing art. Undoubtedly they are good gurus; but that is not enough to make them artists. I would also say that Zen painting rarely does anything for me. I prefer Hokusai, who was a true painter. To be an authentic creator, it is not enough to be a Zen monk who uses impeccable movements to draw little old men laughing. One doesn't have to jumble everything together. I can appreciate a recording of some guru singing a mantra in his deep voice; the fact remains that artistically this guru's singing is a thousand times inferior to the power of an opera singer.

Listening to you I am reminded of the devotional poems that some gurus write, with verses like: "O Lord, in the lotus of my heart, let your grace penetrate." Their disciples

go into ecstasies. It's all very well if the poem corresponds to a real internal experience on the part of its author, but how empty it all seems compared to the least verse of Baudelaire! And I would trade volumes of pious literature for one of Louise Labbé's impassioned love poems. Life melts in her words, in all her erotic tension, unlike the insipid lucubrations of so many so-called spiritual authors.

You see, art has its reasons, which a guru sometimes cannot understand. Art is not ethics; it is aesthetics! It is aesthetic laws and actions, which go far beyond all morals. In my view one cannot arrive at art through mystic searching; but conversely art can lead one on a spiritual quest. An artist can become a guru, unleashing sacred art; I do not believe that a guru can become an artist if he was not already one before his enlightenment.

Can the artistic search and the mystic quest be reconciled? Some people claim that art is no longer interesting to people who are very highly evolved spiritually.

That is not true! I do not believe that at all. What's more, isn't it said of God that he is the great architect of the universe? That is the expression used by the Freemasons, and I even find that too limited. They ought to say simply that God is the great artist. If God were nothing more than an architect, he would not be crazy. Now, God is not logical. I am glad that you have given me the chance to touch on this point, because our era is full of naive creations that are passed off as "spiritual." For me initiatory art starts with an intense quest, an extreme violence, which I had to put in my films just like in my other creations. Once again beauty is convulsive. The universe is an incredible divine convulsion. I don't see why my art should be deprived of this force, emasculated.

In El Topo *you really filmed one man's extreme quest.*

Yes, this man searches for different masters and ends up killing the one he has recognized as his guru. In *Holy Mountain* it's the same. Here you see men who are on a quest for immortality. Before achieving enlightenment they had to traverse their own violence.

According to the "Panic" principle, the artist must implicate himself completely in his work. And so you played yourself in El Topo *and* Holy Mountain. *In* Santa Sangre *your sons played the principal roles.*

With *Holy Mountain* I went through with a certain vision. In *El Topo* I appealed to the actors. But with the next film, I wanted to shoot an initiation. So I went looking for characters just as they were. For example, there was a drugged-up millionaire in my screenplay: I unearthed a businessman addicted to morphine and heroin who had been expelled from the stock exchange after committing enormous fraud. I suggested to this drugged-up millionaire that he could play the role of a drugged-up millionaire. He agreed, for his own amusement. I went to a nightclub to hire two transvestites and to a bar in New York to hire a drunkard. I gathered up the debris of society and offered them a contract to act in my film.

That might be called looking for trouble.

I told them that in order to make the film, they would have to adhere to initiatory discipline and shut themselves up in one house for two months. Then I offered Oscar Ichazo fifteen thousand dollars to come and initiate the group.

What happened?

Ichazo himself only came two times to initiate me personally. For the rest of it, he sent two of his disciples, who worked with the group according to the Arica system for sixty days.

What did the initiation dispensed by Ichazo consist of?

You understand I wanted to come into contact with a guru in order to be able to play that role myself in the film. I was quite surprised when Ichazo told me first to take a shower, then to take an LSD pill, and then to let him guide me on a "voyage."

Was this "initiation" convincing?

It was quite a fundamental experience insofar as I had never taken drugs. I was forty years old and very sober. I did not smoke or drink, and suddenly I was face to face with someone who was pushing me to drug myself in order to have an experience on a new level. I ordered him not to fry my brain, the instrument of my work, and I swallowed the pill. The process was unleashed. I saw my own face on that of Ichazo and felt how much I needed a father. Then he had me walk around my library, and I was immersed in it, so to speak. Then he told me to connect to different centers in myself. I concentrated on my belly and gained access to a multidimensional conception of the world; then to my heart, which I saw as an immense gold cathedral, and felt that it was my own best friend; finally I entered into the void of my brain. This was my preparation for acting in *Holy Mountain*.

And the actors you found? Did they see the light and become "initiates"?

No, they became hams! After six months one who claimed to be a great disciple wept because they didn't bring him his breakfast. The others elbowed each other to get in front of the camera. I realized that film perverts people and cannot lead them to a vision of reality. That is why, at the end of the film, I declare that it's all an illusion, and you can see the cameras filming.

Nonetheless, it's a very good film.

For me it was a failure. But a good failure, an attempt to approach real work.

Holy Mountain and El Topo met with a certain success; they are cult films.

Yes, I withdrew in the midst of my success. *El Topo* is a legendary film in the United States.

The mere fact of getting to the point of filming constitutes the achievement of an enormous work: you have to meet with producers, find the money, compete, direct a crew.

And once you have the crew, get them to do what you want. Yes, it's war. Second after second you risk everything for everything. First you have to fight to ensure production; then locations have to be found; then it is important not to choose the wrong actors; then, once the filming has begun, you have to struggle to get to the goal, overcoming everything: power failures, people's lack of discipline, delays. Finally you have to do the editing, finalize the soundtrack, oversee the sound mixing, and the promotion. It's a titanic task. For a year you can't get sick, get discouraged, or relax your vigilance. In this moment you see me sitting before you and I appear as a normal being. But if you had seen me in Mexico, shouting into a bullhorn, surrounded by eight hundred people! Everyone there called me Adolpho; I behaved like a perfect dictator, never let anything slip by me. During the filming of *Santa Sangre,* I didn't talk with anyone, and I was totally concentrated on the work. My only purely human contact consisted of calling my family once each day. I did not receive any nonprofessional visits, did not allow myself to do any reading. For four months one of my teeth hurt, but I endured the pain because I did not have time to go to the dentist. I finally took an hour off to have it pulled out before continuing the work. Because I did not have great American resources at my disposal, every minute counted. I had to concentrate the time and my efforts in order for the film to succeed.

After completing Holy Mountain *you worked on the adaptation of Frank Herbert's novel,* Dune.

Yes, but that project was not finished.

Even if it was not completed, this project has become no less legendary. A pile of articles have been written about it, and you yourself published a little book about this adventure. The film Dune by Alejandro Jodorowsky does not exist, but the project in itself constitutes a work of art. You received contributions from people of great talent, such as the artist Mœbius, and this embryonic film is a sublime failure, a masterpiece of the uncompleted.

Ultimately, you succeeded in making a sort of "Panic monument" out of this failure.

Yes, in a certain way this unmade film has changed the film industry. I assembled a team of designers and painters who had never done film before. Later they were all asked to work in *Alien,* which was successful, as you know. The ideas that were in the *Dune* project are also very present in *Star Wars* and *Blade Runner.* At the risk of sounding like a megalomaniac—but, once again, why speak ill of myself?—my influence impregnated the whole film industry through the group of people that I assembled and who then worked for Hollywood.

How was this failure for you?

It was a formidable lesson. I really wanted this project to be completed, I worked on it for years, and I envisioned a collective work of an unprecedented initiatory power. In fact, it was because of its profundity that the project finally could not be finished. Hollywood was not ready for this dimension.

You recounted all the events of the preparation in the booklet published by Les Humanoïdes Associés, to which I refer the readers of our interviews. Can you describe to me your collaboration with Mœbius?

At the time that I contacted him, Mœbius was not undertaking any conscious spiritual search. He was suffering profound anguish and was groping around in confusion. This collaboration transformed his life, and he embarked on a true quest. I admire him a great deal because I saw him evolve, unlike other artists who simply destroy themselves little by little. You know, to see if someone is truly a human being, one must follow him on a journey of at least twenty years. Plenty of my friends have died from drinking too much, smoking too much, squandering their energies. Today some are completely decrepit. I, at the age of sixty, feel like I am beginning a new life. Therefore I believe that it is important to keep one's body in good shape, especially if one carries riches within oneself to pass on. Bit by bit, as I have gotten older and progressed in my joyous vision of myself, old age appears to me as a blessing. Age brings me situations that I never could have experienced when I was thirty. Each period of life brings with it a new dimension. Divinity has constructed man as a totality. The duration of our existence is divinely programmed, and one can truly comprehend the work of God only if one has lived the interval of time that corresponds to us. If I am meant to live to be a hundred, it is my duty not to stupidly abridge my life. I can now grasp what a human being is. This is not a matter of protecting oneself out of fear of dying, but out of love and respect for the divine work. To all those young people who say "Why live well, for tomorrow we die," I say that human life is a marvelous initiation. It even goes beyond death; but one dies well only if one has lived well.

Destiny also comes into play. And what if your destiny were to die right now, in an accident?

I believe one makes one's own destiny. Everything that happens to us corresponds to our being. Destiny is created by the ego. For sure there are natural catastrophes, events that modify the course of our lives and are the will of God. Generally speaking I think that the ills of the world are the will of God. All illnesses are collective: if such illness exists, I am ill. If poverty exists, I am hungry. On the other hand, if beauty exists, I am beauti-ful! I have been told the story of a guru who spent the whole day prostrate because he felt all the suffering of the world. If someone was massacred somewhere, he felt it; if there was a famine, he was affected by it. And so he just spent all his time lying down. For me this is only a demi-guru. To be complete he would have also had to feel all the marvels, all the beauty of the world, at the same time as the pain. Because there are still mir-acles on this Earth. I told you that I recently lost an envelope containing fifteen thousand francs in cash at a restaurant I fre-quented regularly. A week later I went back, and the guys there returned the envelope to me with its contents intact. It was a miracle! Likewise, it's a miracle that we are here talking with each other, that a young man like you is interviewing a person like me in order to try and find something good in them. In this conversation the will to find something good comes from you. I respond by showing you the best in myself, in order to satisfy your search. It is nice that such things exist.

Not to fall into too much mutual admiration, but it's also nice that you have confidence in me and that you participate so spontaneously. Because really, we hardly know each other; I proposed these interviews, and you wanted to start them immediately without requiring any sort of guarantee from me. You are not obliged to have faith in me.

I am not obliged . . . but I have nothing to lose.

Aren't there some people in whom you feel confident right away, while others make you suspicious?

Bueno, that's a discerning question. For me no one is truly unknown. By this I mean that when I am face to face with someone for the first time, I perceive his diamond, his inner divinity. I also see to what point that inner divinity is realized or not realized. Looking in his eyes and listening to his voice, I measure his intentions and the foolishness to which he is or is not susceptible. So this is not so much a question of confidence as of what I perceive instantaneously when a person enters into my awareness. Or when I work with someone or do not work with him. It is a choice: yes or no. "To have confidence" implies that one can also be suspicious. And suspicion is a sign of weakness. A samurai does not have confidence in a person. He either acts or does not act with that person, you see? And indeed there are some people with whom I will undertake nothing.

When I'm here in your company, it seems to me as if I've known you forever.

One has this impression in the company of people who have worked on themselves. I'll tell you something banal: if someone works on his own psyche, he is also working on your psyche. The psychical gains of one being benefit all humanity. You have known me forever because you have known yourself forever.

We came to this topic by talking about Mœbius and the way in which he changed, little by little, when he was in contact with you.

You know, when I was involved with the path of consciousness, I told myself: One cannot change the world; but one can begin to change it. One cannot change oneself, but one can begin to change oneself. The marvel is to begin. From then on I resolved to have initiatory conversations with everyone, to always breathe an element of awakening into my creations. I no longer want to deviate from the path. Just as in our interviews, there must always be a transition from the person to the universal, from the banal to the extraordinary. I want nothing for myself that is not for other people. There are no small things in this domain. If I can be the instrument of a very small awakening, I do not hesitate. For example, these last few days, you and I have come to this café. It opened recently, it's very near my house, and I come here almost every day. Several times I asked for tea with lemon, and the owner always said that he didn't have lemons. After drinking tea with milk several times, I had a discussion with him, telling him that he should show a little initiative and go buy a lemon from the grocery store across the street, in order not to lose customers. He thanked me cordially and started serving tea with lemon. Once a week I give lectures near a café in Paris. I advised the owner to start serving mint tea, knowing that my students like to drink it. He followed my advice, and now every Wednesday he gets a good deal of money. These apparently insignificant interventions come from a process that consists of spreading just a little bit more awareness wherever I am. If I happen to talk with someone in the metro, we immediately start to have a profound conversation. We should treat every person who comes to us in this way, addressing the most essential part of the person. There is no need to address thousands of people all at once.

From this perspective the tarot is an important tool for you. When did you begin to be really interested in it?

During the *Dune* period, when I was newly settled back in France. There are a great many different tarots, but for me the only truly sacred one is the Tarot of Marseilles. I began to give courses and consultations and invented the idea of tarot by telephone. In fact, the tarot is a sort of super I Ching: the card proposes a path to the person, who must then decide whether or not to accept what it suggests. There is always a proposition, which, if one accepts it, must then be interpreted.

Each week you give lectures before an attentive audience.

This is how it works: I don't do any advertising; otherwise there would be too many people. People pass on the address by word of mouth. I rent a room, and I tell the audience: "At the exit you must leave me enough money to cover the cost of the room and take my family out to dinner." The attendees therefore pay a little money, which is immediately spent: I pay for the room, then have dinner with my children or with friends I have invited. Two and a half hours after the lecture, I sit in a café, and those who wish to do so come and sit one by one at my table and tell me their problems in five or six minutes. These little consultations are completely free. I respond, sometimes directly, sometimes with the aid of the tarot. From six to eight thirty, I am in a state of complete listening. Then I speak again for two hours. Thus, four or five hours each week are devoted entirely to others.

Do the people who listen to you tend to see you as a master?

Undoubtedly but I always add a comic element. I call the lectures the "Mystic Cabaret" and consider myself the Raymond

Devos of mysticism. I want to be seen, above all, as a well-intentioned human being. My subject is nothing other than holiness, but not that of churches. Every person who truly opens up to another person is in a state of holiness. This is the state that I hope to bring about, in myself and in others who listen to me.

Where do you place sexuality?

In a very important place, insofar as sexuality is the source of all creation. Without sexuality there would be no art, no mysticism, no realization of any kind! But one must know how to use one's sexuality well, to channel it in the direction of creativity and harmonious relations with others. Sexual relations can constitute a path of realization, as long as one always feels that one is staying on that path. If passion diverts you from the path, then that passion is not worthwhile. It must be controlled. From a truly initiatory perspective, amorous relations should not make you deviate from your path but, on the contrary, should favor the concentration of energies that can lead to crystallization. From this viewpoint sexual love is necessary; it has its place in the economy of salvation, so to speak. When people come to talk to me about their sexual problems, my work consists of returning their sex life to the perspective of the path. Sex must happen one way or another; but it should be accomplished on the path in order that the man or woman will not sacrifice him or herself to a passionate relationship.

This morning I read the remarks of a guru who spoke condescendingly of sexuality, seeing it only as miserable animal pleasure. I thought that this was very wrong and

that he was undoubtedly speaking of something he did not know. When integrated in the path, physical love is a subtle and revealing experience.

And moreover why malign the animal in us? Is not the animal divine? Man must tend to the animal within himself. If you have a horse you love it; you respect it; you give it food and drink. Sex is the temple of God. The guru in question must have had garbage between his legs to see such ugliness in sexuality, which is the very energy of creation. We are all born from sex, after all! And what's more, holiness has nothing to do with chastity. I do not see why a saint should not have ten children.

You yourself have followed the yoga of the family; I see you here surrounded by your children.

Oh, I don't think so! In my youth I was rather irresponsible. I had a first child, whom I deserted; then a second, a daughter, whom I also abandoned. Then I met the woman with whom I live today and had three more children with her. I wrote to the mothers of my first two offspring and suggested they send them to me, which is why all my children came to live with me. It was a phrase from Maître Philippe that made me aware of my responsibilities: he said that if one leaves debts in life, one must return to repay them. I asked myself what my debts could be, and realized that they were above all of an emotional nature. My own debts were nothing other than children scattered over the world. From this moment on I became the father of a family. Obviously I could not stay with all the women, but at least I could take care of their children. That is what I did. I could not claim enlightenment without having an enlightened family, without allowing my offspring to follow the same evolution.

The family atmosphere that reigns here appears very agreeable to me. I was struck by it during my first visit.

Oh, it is paradise; we all do what we want. We have our little family quarrels, which is entirely normal, because we each have to express ourselves. But we are very solid. I have seen to it that they each have their own room in which they feel truly at home in their own universe and where they can do what they like without having to reveal it. My oldest son, who has moved out to live with his wife, first lived with her for two years in my house. I was not at all opposed to his having a sexual life in the house of his parents, on the contrary. His wife made a lot of noise when she had orgasms; in my view these cries of pleasure were a blessing for the entire household, and I did not try to prevent my eight-year-old from hearing them. He knew that they were cries of pleasure and welcomed them as something happy and normal. All this has contributed to establishing a very healthy atmosphere. For example, all my children who are old enough to be in a relationship are naturally faithful to their partners.

Do you consider fidelity to be important?

From a certain moment, yes, it becomes extremely important. This does not exclude the experiences of youth, which are undoubtedly necessary. But after that it is fundamental to live on a basis of fidelity. Now, we can also talk about fidelity in relation to metaphysical practice and teaching. In my view a spiritual man, even if he sometimes contradicts himself, is nonetheless following an inner path from which nothing can make him deviate. Without a doubt he adapts externally to circumstances; but these circumstances do not change his inner direction. And above all he does not use teaching to justify his failures. Castaneda, for example, lives by the principle that a warrior leaves no trace; he does not let journalists take his photo and does not profit from his fame by taking the spotlight. On a different note Krishnamurti held to a perfectly consistent position: no disciples, no successor.

Do you try to have such an attitude?

I do not try; I have it! I have always told the people around me that I sprouted like a mushroom, without the least effort. I work a great deal to perfect my artistic creations; I take pains to promote them, because this follows the logic of the media. In my view one must play along with the media if one has something to sell, whether it be a film, a book, a *bande dessinée.* But the spiritual domain obeys other laws. From a spiritual point of view, I have nothing to sell. I am content to act without thinking about the fruits of my action. I give a push, and there it all is! For ten years now I have given lessons every week without the least bit of publicity, and through this I have become a beneficial and useful instrument for hundreds of people.

Among the creations that you have endeavored to "sell" and that also have initiatory significance, the bandes dessinées occupy an important place. How did you begin collaborating with illustrators?

Bueno, I read BDs from my earliest years, in Chile. I was delighted by all the greatest American strips of the golden age: *Flash Gordon, Brick Bradford, Mandrake the Magician, King of the Royal Mounted, The Spirit* by Will Eisner. . . . Ah, so marvelous! The BDs transported me to another world. I loved *Prince*

Valiant, by Foster, for its initiatory aspects relating to the quest for the grail. These strips made a profound impression on me, and as always I was not content with admiring them; I had to take action. That's the way I am—like those aficionados who go to a bullfight and one day end up jumping into the arena to face the bull. So, when I was in Mexico, I went to meet with the editor of the cultural pages of *El Sol de México,* the biggest newspaper at the time, to propose running a weekly BD page. I was very well known as a man of the theater, and my proposition was accepted. This is how, for five or six years, the readers of this newspaper had access to my "Panic Fables."

Were you both storyline writer and illustrator?

Yes, I drew without knowing how to do it . . . I applied myself greatly, so the result was not too bad. Through this strip, which reached a million readers, I was able to transmit all sorts of messages relating to prayer, meditation, Zen, symbolism. . . . Later, in France, it was harder for me to get into the BD milieu. Everything here is more hermetic, and one wastes a lot of time before obtaining the means to create. But during the development of the *Dune* project, I worked day after day with Mœbius. A profound friendship grew between us, and I proposed that we create *The Incal* together. Jean-Pierre Dionnet, who worked with Les Humanoïdes Associés, placed all his confidence in us, and we embarked on this adventure. The storyline came to me during a lucid dream, and I wanted to use BD to show the process of inner transformation.

There again, you envisaged nothing other than an "initiatory" BD.

The BD appeared to me like an unexploited treasure: hundreds of thousands of young people thrive on them, and I saw an undreamed of opportunity to convey the elements of consciousness, to carry out a work of purification. Therefore, I forbade myself any manifestation of my own ego, any depressing approach to life. My topics led toward an awakening; that was all that interested me. Now children and youths love initiatory tales. These strips met with real success, and I continued on my trajectory, with Mœbius as well as other illustrators.

Aren't the great classic strips in the initiatory vein, even unbeknown to their authors? Like fairy tales they are rich in symbols, making use of powerful archetypes.

Absolutely! It's enough to think of Tintin: *The Seven Crystal Balls, Tintin in Tibet.* . . . All the great strips deliver an appeal to consciousness, in a more or less assertive manner. Why? Because at heart a strip author remains more or less a child. I saw my friends hunched over their drawing boards for eight hours a day, fascinated by their work. . . . They fall in love with their characters. They are big children, and a child will always be close to divinity. And the art of a man who is filled with the spirit of childhood will always be alive. For sure, where there is light, shadows reign as well. BDs have gone through a profound decadence. Some have gotten drunk on their success and have gone much too far into insults and rubbish. But we are witnessing a renaissance. Little by little they are returning to storylines built on and suffused with a spirit favorable to awakening.

As a BD author and filmmaker, what connections do you see between the 7th art and the 9th art—as BD are known?*

There are the fine arts and the cinematic arts. But the reader of a BD is mobile, unlike the viewer of a film. By this I mean that a BD is immobile and that it is up to the reader to give it its vitality, its rhythm. He is free to read the album for an hour or for a year. He can retrace his steps back through it, and so forth. Film proceeds in an exactly opposite manner: the spectator is immobilized in front of a work that moves. This means that BD and film are industrial arts that can only survive by reaching a vast audience.

You have also devoted yourself to the more private joy of writing . . .

I published three books in France: a collection of fables titled *Les Araignées sans mémoire,* with Les Humanoïdes Associés; a novel published by Flammarion, *Le paradis des perroquets;* and lastly another novel with Acropole, *Enquête sur un chemin de terre.* In fact, literature interests me a great deal. I think I have about ten fanatical readers . . .

You're joking!

Oh, hardly! In fact, I love writing. When I do it I do nothing else, from morning to night, without stopping. Of all my activities writing is undoubtedly the most wonderful.

Why?

With writing I have no limits. I am my own master. There's no

---

*[It is a French convention to assign numbers to the arts, with architecture normally being the first, sculpture the second, and so forth. —*Trans.*]

one on my back, no producer, no illustrator. . . . Sometimes the editor tries to get involved a little. It's a matter of being open to good suggestions without letting oneself be overwhelmed by the opinions of others. I write in Spanish, a rather rigid Spanish, because I live in France and only speak Spanish with my family, within a closed circle, so to speak. Languages evolve like living individuals. They are rivers that flow. My Spanish is a glass of water. . . . That's all!

Do you know your readers? Do you receive letters from them?

You know, a handful of authentic readers is enough to make one feel understood and to be able to tell oneself that it's worthwhile writing a book. For my last novel two young people from Radio Beur came to interview me, and I saw that they had truly absorbed my book. This was enough for me to be fulfilled. We talked for two hours; then I forgot all about the novel, satisfied at having reached at least two readers. . . . In any case I should make clear: books like mine hardly get beyond two or three thousand copies. Obviously, if I compared this level of success to that of my BD albums, some of which have sold 100,000 copies, there would be good reason to feel disappointed. But one must accept this state of things; that's why I have enormous respect for those writers who persevere, pursuing a profound work without trying to produce bestsellers. Every novel, every profound work is a gift from its author to humanity. The writer invests all his time, all his energy into his creation, knowing that he will gain practically nothing from it. What a magnificent gift! Yes, writers are benefactors to the human species.

Are you a big reader? Your room is crammed with books, and we're talking here in this vast library.

Yes, I read nonstop, whenever I can, particularly at night, until two or three in the morning. I would like to sleep a little more, but there is so much to discover.

I am very intrigued by your way of living, of organizing yourself. Because you do an enormous number of things, yet when I visit you, I feel that you are available, as if you had all the time in the world. This house does not appear subject to rules, to regular schedules; everything seems to happen naturally. Most creative people who produce as much as you stick to a draconian schedule.

You know, when I was working on the *Dune* screenplay, I learned that Frank Herbert had put his wife and children through some real tyranny while he was writing the book, which is certainly a masterpiece. Everyone had to walk around on tiptoe because papa was writing. Learning this made me very sad; I felt a profound pity for these children who had to submit to such a regime. I do not want it to be like that in my house. I've always asked my children not to interrupt me, but I can work in the midst of noise and chaos. I have never asked them to be quiet. It's my job to concentrate. The other day my youngest picked up a guitar and began yelling so loudly that my wife was fed up with it and told him to stop. This upset me, and I told him: "Come sing with me." I yelled along with him for an hour. I understand why my wife was infuriated; that's human. But when my son shouts, I love his voice. I am happy to hear it, even if he is uttering horrible squeaks. I have come to love these vocalizations because I contemplate them from the perspective of eternity, in the presence of my death. Every instant that I spend with my children is a divine moment, a gift from heaven. Sitting down with them to eat breakfast, taking them to see some horror movie that they're crazy about, letting them yell all around me. All this is marvelous; it's an inestimable gift. Their cries are like the songs of the birds in my garden. Why tell a bird to be quiet? Why require my children to walk on tiptoe? Year after year I have gotten used to reading, creating, writing surrounded by noise, by comings and goings. A Persian proverb says: "A drowned man isn't afraid of the rain." I am immersed in what I am doing. How could I be afraid?

The fear of lacking money is one of the most widespread fears among human beings today. Have you ever been unable to meet necessities?

This only happened to me once, about nine years ago. The producer of my film *Tusk* was not very honest, and he did not pay me once the work was finished. I had trusted him, so between one day and the next, I found myself without a cent for my family to live on. I called my friend, the American millionaire Robert Taicher, who gave me a large sum of money, and I jumped into tarology. Until then I had not allowed myself to charge money for teaching the tarot. Necessity required me to do so, and without a doubt this was good for me. At first I was truly ashamed: me, the famous filmmaker who had always gotten his way! But then I realized that I just had a problem with money, that every service had to be paid for, and that I shouldn't get so upset about it. My father always had a certain repugnance for money, which he considered dirty, shameful.

These temporary difficulties gave me a unique opportunity to progress in a domain where I did not feel very much at ease. That being said, apart from this very brief period, I have always been well protected from an economic point of view. That's something verging on the miraculous. Coming from a family of shopkeepers, I have always had a horror of business matters. When someone presents me with a contract, I do not discuss it; I can't even stand to read it all. My goal has always been to create and to leave it to others to sell my creations. I have lived in this way without a problem.

I feel rich insofar as I have what I need, and I am free to create.

Your relationship with money is quite singular. I'm thinking of those envelopes full of cash that you carry around.

Yes, I often go out with a large amount of cash in my pocket: fifteen or twenty thousand francs. For me it's a sort of magic ritual. The other day, as you know, I lost that envelope containing fifteen thousand francs in cash in the café where I normally go before my lectures. Upon realizing it I told myself: "I am rich! Rejoice at losing money, for only he who has it can lose it!" I reflected: Here I am with fifteen thousand francs less, and yet my life has not changed. I continue eating and living. Consequently I am rich.

That what's known as a positive attitude!

Even better it was a week later that I went back and asked about it, just to set my mind at rest, without expecting anything, and I felt perfectly calm. To my great surprise the waiters at the café had kept the envelope, and they gave it back to me intact, with all its contents. I gave them three thousand francs, because it seemed fair to reward them for their honesty. Generally speaking one must pay one's debts, take care to give back to others what they have given you. That is a law. This is why, when I gave my little free consultations at the café, I asked each person to symbolically trace the words "thank you" with a finger on the table once the interview was finished.

It is also interesting to observe how some people had a lot of trouble giving thanks, making this simple gesture. It would undoubtedly have been easier for them to give money. It is a great misfortune to be incapable of giving thanks. A mystic must be able to express his gratitude. True prayer is an action of gratitude and not of asking for something. I am unceasingly thankful for everything that has been given to me. A bodhisattva blesses every person who enters his field of vision.

Your field of vision also extends into the domain of dreams. I believe you attach quite a lot of importance to dreams.

Indeed. Transpersonal psychologists have not yet gotten past the stage of the lucid dream. But it is possible to go further. When I was nineteen I was lucky enough to have my first lucid dream, which was particularly memorable. I was in a cinema, and I had to get out. I was conscious of my dreaming state, and it seemed to me that I absolutely had to wake up, because I knew I would die if I left by a certain door. I made an enormous effort, felt myself rise up out of the darkness toward the surface, and returned to waking consciousness. I have never been able to forget this experience, and I have reflected a great deal upon the fear that seized me in the dream. After all why did I think I would die if I left? I could just as well have gone out the door and visited whatever was on the other side. Over the years I have had more and more lucid dreams. At first, once I knew I was dreaming, I gave myself over to various experiences. For a time I sought out sexual adventures; the orgies in which I ended up quickly made me lose control. After that I sought out money; that had the same result. My point here is that each time I pursued a crude, nonspiritual goal, the dream took control of me, and I sank into a sleep that was devoid of any consciousness. Once I identified with the elements of the dream, I let myself get wrapped up in them and lost all lucidity.

This is something very symbolic and a rich lesson for waking life as well.

Later I embarked on a quest for the inner god, who presented himself to me in the form of a giant academic, a supreme professor. This was merely the projection of my own ego. Finally, as I made gradual progress in the domain of lucid dreams, I was subject to another phenomenon, which, in my view, is more far-reaching, and which I call the humble dream, full of wisdom and humanity. The actions I carry out in dreams are accurate, perfect. I become what I am at the absolute depths of myself, which is to say, a sage. I stop wanting to control the outcome of the dream, and I abandon myself to it totally, with the certainty that everything is perfect. In the lucid dream one wants to be the demiurge, one usurps the role of God. In the humble dream, by contrast, one renounces all control, no longer chasing after power. One no longer feels the desire to be a warrior, to shape one's destiny. One understands that the subconscious is a universe, within which one is to play a small role and play it perfectly. Then the dreams become something of great beauty, devoid of anguish. One finds oneself in one's place, no longer at the center of events, but as a witness. I have never spoken of these experiences before. Without a doubt the time has come, because in my view the humble dream constitutes a great hope. It is the point at which the subconscious stops sending us negative images; nightmares no longer happen. Another characteristic of this type of dream is that one always finds oneself to be unified. One never carries out the least action without being totally in agreement with oneself.

Has your waking life been influenced by this?

Yes, I live tranquilly. I know that one can seek to obtain no greater treasure than inner joy and peace.

Alejandro, are you happy?

Yes, I feel tranquil. Whatever may happen I feel good.

Are you a sage?

An ape? [*singe*]

A sage! (laughter)

Ha ha ha! I prefer to say that I am an ape! Ha ha ha! You know, it is difficult to apply such a term; one runs the risk of falling into the abyss of words. What is a sage? Really, perhaps I have just been lucky. I have never been seriously ill; my children are all good to me; I have never had to deal with serious problems. Life has been good to me: I never served in the military and only began very late to pay taxes. I have never worked but have always done what I enjoyed, meeting with relative success each time.

My existence is full of favorable coincidences: One day I was in the United States and I needed to renew my visa. At the consulate they told me I could only have a thirty-day visa, which prevented me from traveling, from coming and going as I pleased. It was agreed that I would come back the following day to pick up this one-month visa. The next day, when I showed up, a bomb had exploded at the consulate, and amid the general confusion they gave me a two-year visa! You see, everything happens like this. I have never known war, revolution, grave crises. I settled in France, the calmest country in the world. I did not end up in Lebanon or South Africa, but in a protected location. The monsoon stopped when I filmed *Tusk,* the rains ceased during the filming of *Holy Mountain.* At the age of sixty, I feel that so far I have been spared from everything!

Do you believe that life is good to you insofar as you are good to it? Because ultimately your attitude constitutes a rare positivity! If it is true that our being attracts the circumstances of our existence . . .

I do not know, but in any case I am thankful. I feel a profound gratitude. Having been given the protection from which I have benefited thus far, I do not feel authorized to claim to be a sage. I am someone who has been lucky, and I behave like a sage because life treats me well. I do not know how I would feel if life were less merciful to me. And sometimes I ask myself: What good is it to be a sage? What good is it to become a saint? I feel at ease everywhere. I feel the good around me; I spend all day in a state of concentration. What's more, why should I want to be an artist, to be recognized worldwide? Things either happen or they don't happen. For example, I never sought to gain success from BD; but today I am able to live off them.

You have also had difficulties, failures, and disappointments, like everyone else; but it's your inner attitude that transforms these ordeals into blessings, such as the way in which you made the Dune failure into a work of art.

Perhaps. A Persian proverb says: "If the thief must come at the end of the night, make him come at the beginning of the night." Thus, each woman who left me did me a great service: she relieved me of a person who did not love me! It was good that I was abandoned at that moment and not later on. In fact, in the emotional life, nothing has truly affected me, insofar as everything that has happened to me has been good.

At the age when many people retire, you say you feel like you are beginning a new life. How do you picture your old age?

Each instant is an eternity. If I get five more years, what a marvel! If I get ten or twenty or thirty, what joy! Each new moment that is granted is received as a gift. As for physical decline it happens, to a lesser or greater degree, and that's inevitable. But the spirit can still become more refined. I have never felt more awake than today. When one works on oneself, one has vanquished one's demons, gotten past certain things, and one finds oneself ready to welcome old age with joy.

And if you had to give up this life you love so much right now? Would you accept it?

Certainly, because I have been prepared for it for a long time!

In fact, I would love for my children to see me die, in order that they could understand that death is not something frightening. It should be a great celebration.

In your view what will happen to Alejandro Jodorowsky after his death?

I am not at all curious about it: what will happen will happen, and I accept it in advance! If I sink into nothing, it will be a delicious nothing; if I dissolve into totality, very well! And if I rise from the dead, that will be marvelous. I accept it in advance, because in any case what will happen will happen. So why worry about it? Why give in to anxiety? One day I was in New York for a film, and my producers put a large car with a chauffeur at my disposal. We drove around the city, and I felt a little anxious. The city weighed upon me, with its noises, its frenzy, its movement. So I asked the chauffeur to take me around the business district, Wall Street. I asked him to drive slowly, and I put myself into a state of meditation and became the invisible man, the nonexistent man, the nothing, and everything became a jewel. Everything seemed to me like a dance: the polluted air, the businessmen in a hurry, the lights, the noises. I understood that my anxiety came from a purely animal instinct of self-preservation. Once I became pure nonexistent consciousness, creation, even with its horrors, was unveiled as an emanation from God. I entered into the divine gaze, relieved of my individual existence, and all was well. It is so, what more can I say?

THREE

POSTSCRIPT

Somewhere on this old planet, amid the infinite ecstatic milieus that populate the universe, a man who is almost old is talking with a man who is almost still young.

The almost young man asks the almost old man questions, pretending not to know the answers, and the latter answers, pretending to know the answers.

But the respondent knows that he who knows is he who asks and that ignorance lives in the answer.
How beautiful. This reminds me of those intense rainy nights in Santiago de Chile, where we ate *picarones en almibar*—circles of flour fried in hot sugar—in the cafés at the end of the world.

We ate to make the cold pass by, to make our lives pass by, navigating toward the other world where all questions would receive the same answer.

ALEJANDRO JODOROWSKY

PART TWO

The Path of Goodness

FOUR

TRICKERY
The Return—1989–2004

Fifteen years have passed by since that day when I first followed the path of the Boulevard de la Libération to Vincennes for my first meeting with Jodorowsky. Even if the "man who is almost old," who had just turned sixty then, is now a septuagenarian just five years away from that "great age" of eighty, one would not dream of describing him as "old," considering his intact creativity and spirit.

As for the "man who is almost still young" who had just turned thirty, he has disappeared, leaving in his place a man in his forties. "Jodo" no longer lives in Vincennes, but in Paris proper, not far from the Gare de Lyon. He no longer lives in a house with a garden, but in a large apartment; however, I find that the owner transports his atmosphere wherever he goes. By his side henceforth there is a woman, Marianne, with whose support he continues to lead an existence as vast as always.

This time there is no frenzy surrounding the meeting. This new encounter with Jodo does not take place, like my first encounter, amid an atmosphere of "panic." My instruments of communication have not been stolen, I am not moving, there are no mad telephones, no murky negotiations in shady bars, no garbage bag to be retrieved in a phone booth. Private life—Jodo's as well as my own—is equally tranquil.

In fifteen years we have each loved, suffered, matured. Life has taken from us and given to us. And we have each remained faithful to what was essential to us.

Therefore, we are able to pick up our conversation where we left off.

As Jodo recalls during our interviews, *La Tricherie sacrée* was a sort of miracle, a magical little book in its advent as well as in its consequences. A miracle cannot be reproduced at will.

However, this new edition gives us the opportunity to deliver the news and take stock of things, so to speak.

The neighborhood around the Gare de Lyon in Paris lies beneath the semitwilight of a late winter afternoon. Within the shelter of a bourgeois apartment building, two old friends reunite, in the presence of their respective wives, and take up the thread of an old conversation.

FIVE

DIALOGUE—2003

Listen, Gilles, I'll suggest something to you: let's take the little book [*La Tricherie sacrée*], open it up, and you can ask me exactly the same questions.

All right, let's do something close to what you propose, but not exactly to the letter.

As you wish. The important thing is that we do it now, right?

Exactly, here and now. So, Alejandro, what we are about to attempt now, talking again, fifteen years later, is something like a return of La Tricherie sacrée. What inspired you about this project? As a man of the cinema, you're well aware that the sequel is often not as good as the original film.

Yes, but not always. Consider, for example, *The Godfather,* a series of three marvelous films. The best one is the second! Also, I prefer not to see life as a circle that repeats itself while constantly degrading, but as a spiral that goes toward what is better. From this point of view, if we return to it, it can only go better. Provided that we have worked during the interim!

Exactly. Do you feel that you have worked during the last fifteen years?

As for me, I am like the universe. I tell you this without any megalomania, because it's simply normal. Like the universe I am in perpetual expansion. What interests me a great deal is to see myself grow old. It's like sitting on a riverbank with my feet in the water and watching it flow along. I watch the river of my life pass by and ask myself whether my capacities are diminishing in any way.

And are they?

I have realized, with joy, that the current idea of old age is a prefabricated concept; it serves only to make us exit life as quickly as possible. You see, from the economic point of view, it is better for one to die without too much delay, in order to reduce the cost to pension funds, Social Security, etc. By this logic envisaging old age as horrible decrepitude is the best way to bring about a quick decline. But I contemplate my old age without fear: I am very content in it. My comprehension appears to me ever clearer; my impression is that I am not declining, but progressing. My capacities are not diminishing. Physically I feel the same, not any more tired today than yesterday. Sexually I am not at all the same because today I am faithful!

So something has changed there!

I don't know if it's because I have finally found my life partner or because I no longer have the energy. Well, I believe the first reason is the better one. Certainly the quantity of sperm diminishes. I used to have a lot; today I have a little less each time. But this does not hinder the simple pleasure of having sexual relations with the woman of one's life.

So I cannot complain! This whole story of "Viagra" is a myth. The truth is that some men are lacking love, and that is why they cannot function sexually anymore. When one loves life continues, and no medication can ever be a substitute for love. From the emotional point of view, I have discovered a freedom that I never knew before.

Explain that to me.

I was much too preoccupied with myself: what happened to me, what I wanted, what I felt, my memories, my history, all that. Today, I feel more free from myself, and I have discovered goodwill in this freedom. Goodwill toward all that exists, has existed, will exist. An infinite love for this life that is so ephemeral, that is what one discovers emotionally when one ages well! And from the intellectual point of view, one understands many things better. Ha ha ha! I now have the impression that I am able to solve the secret koans, which used to be pure mystery to me. The sensation of mystery that I used to feel when reading a haiku is no longer there; I now have the feeling that it is speaking to me about something familiar.

And death, Alejandro, has that become familiar too?

Certainly it has begun to establish itself as a constant presence.

You see that you are going to die; you know it. I am not speaking of initiatory death, death to oneself, which is something entirely different, but of death in the ordinary sense. So you begin to vibrate more and more in life because you sense that the spark is in the process of burning out, and each day brings you closer to death. This feeling is good, because with old age useless things lose their importance.

What things would you now classify as useless?

Triumph, success, seduction, wealth. It is wonderful to feel more and more free from all that. It is also wonderful to feel the ephemeral character of this body, which does not belong to me.

What a great step it is to perceive it as a marvelous vehicle that has been loaned to me! And then you begin to see that the mind is also ephemeral. It is the privilege of the body merely to be temporary. In general one distinguishes the mind from the body. The body is supposedly mortal, the mind eternal, so people seek out of fear to take refuge in the values of the mind. But little by little one perceives things in a more real manner; one understands that the mind is no less ephemeral than the body. This realization of the transient nature of the mind, like that of the body, brings about the alchemical wedding: the mind and body are married, and they wait together patiently for their demise, ha ha ha! It's an agreeable impression: instead of feeling alone and afraid at facing the coming extinction, the body knows it will be accompanied by the mind. The two can thus wait together in tranquility. From this one understands that beneath this body and mind that pass away, there is the king's diadem, the red diamond, the inner god, the golden eye: a principle in us that is situated absolutely outside the ephemeral.

Is that what you perceive today?

Yes, I am talking from experience; there is nothing theoretical in my statements.

This is what I experience at nightfall. Each night everyone here goes to sleep: the five cats, my wife, even the telephone stops ringing. Then I stretch out on the bed and let something come, the importance of which I did not know for a long time.

When I knew the Zen master Ejo Takata, he showed me an inscription on a wall: a single word, "happiness." I did not know that he was showing me the essence of Zen in a single gesture. At the absolute depths the secret of life is happiness. And happiness is a state that one refuses due to all sorts of tensions.

Each night I let happiness come into each one of my cells, into my bones, my flesh, my mind . . . I welcome the sensation of happiness.

To gain access to this happiness, one must enter into a condition of not-hoping. When one renounces hope one escapes from fear, and when one escapes from fear, one attains happiness. So this is what I do every night: I lie in bed in a state of re-creation, I become a being made of happiness, and nothing more can happen to me.

In the old days you worked a great deal on dreams. In Le Théâtre de la guérison *we talked at length about lucid dreams. Have these practices helped you to achieve what you know today?*

Yes, certainly. At the beginning I was mainly trying to change my dreams; then, in a second stage, I was content to watch the dream happening, as a spectator. Then I asked myself: What good is that? If one has confidence in one's subconscious, if one views it as an ally, one must let things happen as they come. I stopped having nightmares and had only what I call happy dreams. These are dreams in which I am simply content. Oh, they are stupid sometimes.

Tell me about that.

I can tell you about last night, ha ha ha! So, last night, in my dream, I was putting on a concert with Michael Jackson.

You call that a happy dream?

Why, yes, I felt very good. There was an audience, Michael Jackson, and I, reciting children's poems. Michael was holding invisible children by the hand. He said: Now we will really talk. I composed poems for these children; then he threw himself into my arms and wept with emotion. And I was very content! Then we played our concert. It was silly, but happy.

Another thing is that in my dreams I am no longer ashamed of myself. In my dreams I am exactly the same as I am when I am awake. What I find good in the waking state, I also find good in the dreaming state. There is no difference anymore between the dream personality and the real personality. This makes me profoundly happy.

To feel truly content is a privilege, isn't it?

A privilege of old age, without a doubt, ha ha ha! You know, the brain is like a universe in expansion. I do not believe in its decadence, but on the contrary believe that it only becomes more and more open, acquiring the capacity to integrate more and more as time goes on. For sure the brain as an organ may become fatigued with age, forget details, but this is of no great importance. I am speaking of a greater brain than what one sees by opening up the skull. We do not know what lapse of time is given to us on this Earth; but whatever its duration may be it is a time of maturation, of expansion rather than contraction.

One goes through degrees. What one is capable of seeing at the age of seventy is more vast than what one can envisage at sixty; what one perceives of reality at sixty is broader than what one perceives at fifty; and so forth. In fact, one never stops developing. This is why, in the view of the ancient peoples, old age was respectable. Old people were not considered decrepit people; on the contrary they were seen as human beings who had reached an advanced stage of development and from whom a great deal could be learned. Indeed this view of old age was part of a normal perspective on life. In any case, as far as I'm concerned, at the age of seventy-four, I am almost old and entirely content.

In fact, I do not feel old. Seventy-four years, what does that mean from the inner point of view? I am every age at once.

You are approaching old age in a country that is not the one where you were born. Does this in any way influence how you feel inwardly?

If age is relative then so is nationality. What is my nationality? Inside myself I have no nationality, I swear! Not to say that I dislike Chile, where I was born; but I do not feel any patriotic roots apart from my belonging on this planet. Along these same lines, at the moment that I am speaking to you, I have no sex; I am androgynous. I have realized that one's way of thinking is strongly determined by one's sex: there is a masculine way of thinking, against which women have reasonably revolted, trying to impose a specifically feminine way of thinking.

All this is very limited, and the awareness of this limitation has led me to research androgynous thinking: a way of thinking that is not determined by sexuality. My investigations of primitive tribes have shown me that we ourselves are primitive, stuck in a masculine way of thinking. In terms of thought we are still troglodytes, psychological barbarians! This is why it is essential to develop an androgynous way of thinking within oneself.

However androgynous your thinking may be, you are still in a man's body and not a woman's.

Of course, but even from this point of view, it is possible to evolve, to identify oneself less. I do not wear any ornament, no ring or watch. I have only one or two suits, one pair of shoes. Not due to poverty, but because these things seem useless to me. In any case the body does not belong to me; it is on loan. It does not horrify me at all that it will be burned, left to rot in the ground, or given to dogs to eat.

It doesn't matter much to me what will happen to my body once I have given it back!

Would you describe yourself today as being detached?

Good question: To what am I still attached? I am privileged, that is certain. I have a career that allows me to be free from financial worries. A career that is both noble and childish, consisting of making "comics."

You mean bandes dessinées?

Yes, "comics"! To be a maker of "comics" is a noble trade because I amuse people and because I make positive things happen in my stories. I am lucky enough not to depend on any government, and I am completely free in my movements. If I wanted to go to China tomorrow, nothing would prevent me. So I enjoy freedom in time and space.

Do you feel attached to your family?

Not in the habitual sense. I have built a very tight-knit family. But with time my children have grown. They are all over thirty, even forty. So I no longer feel linked to them in the same way. I identify myself neither with the father nor with the grandfather that I am.

And yet you still play the roles of father and grandfather?

Yes, I have children and grandchildren, but I do not feel that I am restricted to one family—*my* children, *my* grandchildren. My family is the human race. To go along with the flow of the moment is to go along with the planet, with all other humans. I am not concerned only with certain persons who are linked to me genetically, but with the whole, because this whole is in me. And from this point of view, my main enemy today is petroleum.

Why petroleum?

Our society has come to revere this demonic combustible, which poisons the atmosphere, infests the economy, and unleashes wars. Human beings ought to fight against petroleum, require new and more innocent sources of energy to be used, and leave the petroleum in the Earth; it is the Earth's pith. The discovery and utilization of new energy sources goes hand in hand with the development of consciousness.

How does this happen?

Just as there are belts in karate, there are different levels of consciousness. Animal consciousness, infantile consciousness, adult consciousness, androgynous consciousness.

Divine consciousness?

That I do not believe one can attain, precisely because it is divine, and we are only human. One may approach it, but it is not for us. However, if our consciousness undergoes a transformation, we will find a new energy source, which must already be there, though we are incapable of seeing it.

It is a little like what happens on the individual scale: if one works on oneself, one transforms oneself, one changes, and one gains access to new energies.

I have an example before my eyes.

Yes, you! You have changed. You are not the man I knew. There has been a transformation, but the butterfly you have become should give thanks to the caterpillar.

All your creations—film, theater, literature, bandes dessinées—excuse me, "comics"!—have always had this transformation of the being as their essential theme, right from the beginning.

It's true. I have been greatly drawn to disciplines that are despised.

Today "comics" are considered an art and taken seriously as such, but when I first began to take an active interest in them, they were mocked! As for the tarot let's not go there, esotericism of the lowest caliber. But I know that the lotus grows in the mud, and that is why I love using discredited materials to evoke this essential transformation of which you speak. For example, my film *El Topo,* which the Americans consider an alchemical work, is presented as a cowboy film. It's an initiatory western. I start with a material that is not considered noble, and I transmute it. This is my artistic work.

Can you take this farther and explain what an artist is to you?

What is generally called art consists of the more or less talented representation of subjective problems: I love Kafka, Dostoevsky, and Proust, but that doesn't mean they aren't great neurotics. Great geniuses and great neurotics! As for me, I have always searched for the truth. From the beginning I believed that it was expressed through words; then little by little as I progressed, I realized that I had to cross a frontier, make the extreme sacrifice of articulated language in order to enter the unthinkable. Because the truth is unthinkable. It can be sensed, but one cannot think it. Poetry, art, and beauty lead us to the edges of this unthinkable. Beauty, in a way, is the aura of truth. One cannot see truth, but beauty is visible. The artist's role, therefore, in my view, is to make beauty visible as a reflection of truth. Now beauty assumes that one is recovering from illness; it comes about through healing. Outside of healing it is not real beauty. A viper is beautiful, but its beauty is deceptive because it poisons you. Certain aspects of illness can even fascinate us and therefore appear beautiful to us. Nevertheless, the beauty that heals must be distinguished from the beauty that kills.

However, the beauty that heals incorporates elements of that which kills; seeing your films and reading your

"comics," one does not have the impression of viewing a "new age" artistic expression that allows only pastel colors, unicorns, and good feelings; your creations are not exempt from monsters and violence. The shadow is present as well as light.

Certainly! Alchemy begins with dissolution, putrefaction, calcination, and thus, conflict. Then come evaporation, coagulation, and so forth. Art is an alchemical process. Before arriving at the expression of beauty, one must manifest the difficulties, the tensions. If one attempts to short-circuit the shadows to arrive directly at beauty, one produces an art of rosewater, without density or substance. An art exempt from conflict is an art without history and, therefore, without anything at stake. Consequently you are right to ask me to explain it. For me this is not a matter of achieving an art that is supposedly "pure," which would expel the development process and the shadows. On the contrary I insist on the necessity to not remain in illness; one must make art into a way of healing rather than a morbid indulgence in abnormality. Art is a great path, which I have followed.

Because we are reviving La Tricherie sacrée, *could you tell me, looking back fifteen years, what repercussions this little book has had for you?*

This little book has had fairly great repercussions. At first I experienced its apparition as something a bit magical. It's true, you came to see me; I did not know you at all. I therefore saw a young man arriving at my house and saying to me: "Could we perhaps make a book together?" Since I love to play, I answered: "Yes, let's make this book now!" And then we began to talk, in front of a tape recorder in my library in Vincennes. I expected nothing special: you were there; I thought you were nice; I wanted to talk with you. And then you came back several times, we kept going, your cassette got stolen at the bar near my house, and you retrieved it.

I told about all this in the introduction.

Yes, but what I am saying is that bizarre events surrounded the creation of this little book. You were young, nervous, completely different from how you are today, and you often came there with a different woman. Then one day, some months later, you arranged to meet with me in a café in Paris, and you gave me a very fine little book, all finished! It was magical! We talked without any plan, took things as they came, but the book was clear, limpid, and funny!

So, magic was already there, in the apparition of that little book.

Immediately it made me friends. Many people approached me and were interested in what I did. And then, since this had all gone so well, I pestered you to do *Le Théâtre de la guérison,* and this book changed my life. *La Tricherie sacrée* had already made me known to myself as a creator engaged in a process different from that of an egomaniacal artist.

All the same, Alejandro, you were already very well known before that.

Yes, but only in certain circles. My name appeared in the history of theater because I founded the "Panic" movement with Arrabal and Topor. I was a cult filmmaker known to certain film buffs, and I'd had success as an author of "comics." Some regulars came to my "Mystic Cabaret" and had their tarot cards read. But *La Tricherie sacrée* seemed to unify all these aspects, presenting no longer the various sides of my work but the initiatory spirit, the inner guidance that presides over everyone. Then *Le Théâtre de la guérison* created demand. The people came to me to practice psychomagic. Starting with *Le Théâtre de la guérison,* I was able to develop *The Dance of Reality.* So *La Tricherie sacrée* marked the beginning of a new cycle for me, a new dynamic. At the time that I met you, the entire part of my activity that one could describe as therapeutic took place in the realm of mystery. There was nothing truly public. With *La Tricherie sacrée* it began to be revealed in plain sight. What's surprising is that this happened, so to speak, by itself. Nothing was premeditated! We met, and this little book came into being.

The world is made up just as much of what does not happen as of what does happen. Certain things take place; others could but do not. They are no less present in the state of potential, so one must not regret that they do not happen. If they do not take place, it is because the moment has not come.

La Tricherie sacrée, and then *Le Théâtre de la guérison,* which resulted from it, came about because it was the right time.

And what you or I did not do, but might have done, will be done by others when the time is right. Therefore, I am completely optimistic.

You have published an autobiography titled The Dance of Reality; but my impression is that this expression also refers to a kind of work that you offer to do.

Yes, absolutely. I should explain that I only see people once a week, and for free, on Wednesdays. This begins with a dinner to which I invite a few young poets to the Middle-Eastern restaurant below my apartment.

Is this the Dead Poets Society?

If you like! It's a dinner of young poets. I choose a few young poets and pay them to eat. It's nice to invite people out, right? Then I read the tarot in a café that is also near where I live.

Is this for free also?

Yes, yes. Sometimes I even give out money.

Yes, I sometimes give small sums of money to people for whom I read the tarot. I pay them! Believe me, for them it is a shock. A therapeutic shock. In psychoanalysis it is essential to set a price; as for me, I try to work for free, reserving the possibility of paying my clients now and then, ha ha ha! The other day an Israeli scientist named Yohav reminded me of a story: at the end of a tarot workshop, I declared to the participants that I had learned a great deal from them, so I gave them their money back. I remember having done something similar at a bookshop in Paris. You were there, correct?

Oh yes! A memorable evening!

This esoteric bookshop had organized a viewing of my film *Holy Mountain,* at the end of which I had to take the floor and speak with the audience.

Now I thought that the organizer was charging a very high price for the event. Not only was her price too high, but she was not paying me enough of a percentage! So I decided to teach her a lesson. When I arrived at the beginning of the evening to give her the videotape of the film, I told her: "Okay, the money you are giving me for this evening, you cannot give it to me a week from now, you cannot give it to me tomorrow, you must give it all to me right after the film ends, otherwise I will not speak." She answered: "But I have to sort the cash in the register; I have to count the money; that takes time." I retorted: "The film lasts two hours; you have two hours to count."

So two hours later I came back, and she had spent the duration of the film with her nose buried in her money. She paid me, then I got up in front of the audience and declared: "Look here, I have a problem. I am very annoyed. I never give lectures with admission charges. Only free lectures! And now I learn that you have paid, and paid a high price, to attend this event. So I find myself in a dilemma. The organizer has given me a very small percentage. It's my film, I am putting on the event, and I am not earning much. I've had enough of this spiritual business! I've had enough of poor gurus like myself being exploited! And so, I see only one solution for my peace of mind: I will give you your money back."

At this moment, the organizer began protesting: "But you can't do that! Some people have paid less than others because they have season tickets, etc., etc." I answered: "No problem. I will reimburse each person one by one; it will be a big party!" I believe that on that evening, through this act, I taught her a lesson about her attachment to money. Note that I didn't give her share back; I only gave back my share. She gave nothing back. She wasn't stupid. That said one must sometimes be stupid and know how to lose. Consider my partner, Marianne, for example: She is very intelligent and much younger than I am. With her I have learned to let myself be conquered. I let her do what she wants, I surrender, and that goes very well. From time to time one must know how to surrender, how to not always impose one's will. However, there are also plenty of occasions when one must not surrender. It is a delicate equilibrium: knowing how to surrender most of the time in order to be in charge when necessary.

At least this is how I see things, at the risk of being mistaken.

Do you believe you are often mistaken?

Even the pope makes mistakes! So, yes, I risk being mistaken. I am not afraid of it, because what good is it to fear the inevitable? I only try to be mistaken as little as possible, knowing that however rarely it happens I am not infallible. Once I was at the Vatican attending a ceremony. The pope appeared at the balcony. A dove flew close to him. He backed away, then shooed it off! Undoubtedly he was afraid the dove would crap on his white habit. But you can imagine the catastrophe: in front of a crowd of people expecting to see the Holy Spirit descend, the pope brushes off a dove that descends onto him! In my view, on that day, the pope made a mistake. He should have let the dove land on his head while he talked. If I had seen the dove land on his head, I would have been converted immediately. All this is just to say that one may always be mistaken.

I suppose that you take care to make as few mistakes as possible when you read the tarot, because in this situation you exercise a great deal of responsibility. Your words have weight.

First of all, in order to read the tarot, I have to be feeling good. If I feel bad I cannot read it. I must also enter into contact with the goodness inside me. Every therapeutic act—and the reading of the tarot is one—consists of applying infinite goodwill to the other person. This therefore requires the elimination of all judgment with regard to the other. One must accept the person exactly as she is, just as one accepts a cat as it is.

If it never occurs to us to criticize a cat, then why criticize a person?

You advise certain people who come to you for tarot readings to find a spiritual master, often Arnaud Desjardins. Can you talk about this?

What I am about to say should not be misinterpreted—that is, interpreted superficially—but in a certain manner: I use Arnaud as one of my instruments. First I met him—at your place, fifteen years ago. Then I went to visit him at his ashram in Ardèche. And I noticed that I was in the presence of a man who was 100 percent honest, which is quite rare! I would say that we recognized each other in our honesty. We are very different, we act differently, we do not have exactly the same role; but even if he has his vision of things and I have mine, beyond the differences on the surface, his honesty meets with mine, and vice versa. We are brothers in honesty.

In a chord there are three notes, and the notes are different, but together they make a chord. I feel that Arnaud and I form a chord. Because he carries out the function of master, he fulfills the role of the absent father. When people come to me who have neither master nor god—in my view, to be without a god is to be ill—and who are alone in their existence, without a father, then I send them to a spiritual man. I do not want to send them to a Chinese, Tibetan, or Japanese spiritual man, because they are French, or in any case they are European. In my view Arnaud carries out a formidable task, healing family trees and appeasing empty and errant spirits.

It is up to him to decide whether or not to receive those I send to him, but I make this suggestion to certain people for whom I feel that it will turn out to be beneficial. It is in this sense that Arnaud Desjardins becomes a tool for healing that I try to use on the people who come to me.

It's not irreverent, it's true! Ha ha ha!

And since you are now working with Arnaud, I also send people to you, as a younger instructor. In fact, I rely on many allies in my healing work. One day I heard a story about Buddha: He was asked to heal an insufferable person, but things did not go well at all between him and this person, who detested him. So he said to himself: this woman is not for me to heal, but for my son. He sent her to his son, who healed her. If Buddha can't heal everything, neither can I. Therefore, I must have allies, and that is how I view Arnaud. I hope he will not be offended by this.

Do you have other "allies" of this kind?

I also have an ally in karate: a formidable karate master, to whom I send those who I believe have a true need to practice a martial art, in order to discharge their violence and find their center. His name is Jean-Pierre Vignaud. He's a magical man. He broke his pelvis into seven pieces and was lame for seventeen years! During all that time he was truly lame, waiting to be operated on until the surgical technique was perfected. Now it's done, and he can walk. But lame or not he never stopped being what he is: a karate master. For me he is an ally who embodies the will to heal. Faced with certain maladies I send people to a psychotherapist, Jean-Claude Lapraze. I have a whole list of auxiliaries whom I use, sometimes without them knowing. Because the world is mine, the masters are also mine! They are part of the world, and I can use them, ha ha ha!

Let's talk about your films. When I met you you were already a cult filmmaker, notably of El Topo *and* Holy Mountain. *Shortly after* La Tricherie sacrée, *you directed* The Rainbow Thief, *a curious film that takes place in a sewer, with an impressive cast: Omar Sharif, Peter O'Toole, and Christopher Lee.*

Yes, *The Rainbow Thief.* A well-intentioned work, but ultimately done mostly to earn a living. I wanted to have the experience of making a big-budget film, to know what it's like to be the director of a thirteen-million-dollar production! It was an experience. The scriptwriter was the wife of the producer, they quarreled, the film was cut, and in the end it was never shown in the way I had conceived it. There was an irreconcilable conflict between them: he wanted nothing but action; she wanted nothing but text. He cut the script; she cut the action.

So it was difficult to achieve anything! One day who knows what will happen, because all the material is there: a DVD, perhaps.

At the time you told me some lovely stories about your unconventional relationship with the stars.

Ha ha ha! I had the good and the bad. The good was Omar

Sharif the bad was Peter O'Toole. You understand, this film was a business enterprise, and I was the employee of the production. When I make a film like *Holy Mountain,* I am the creator, the poet, my role is central. But in the making of an industrial film, the director is a slave. The master is the star. So when the star arrives, he begins by having a fit of rage to indicate that he is the one in charge and that you are at his service. So right at the beginning, when Omar Sharif arrived, his great tyrannical childish rage flared up. These star tantrums are always without a valid reason, but that doesn't matter much; the spoiled child has to have his fit. Well, I'm not used to people manipulating me in this way. I'm not a Hollywood valet. So I got angry. He yelled at me so much that I decided not to speak to him at all anymore. I picked up a stick and brandished it under his nose, telling him that if he kept yelling I would break his head. Then I stopped talking to him directly. I went through my assistant. I told my assistant what Omar Sharif had to do, and the assistant went and told him. After two or three days of this regime, he cracked. He came to me and said: "Come, come, let's be friends, let's stop this." From then on we became great friends, truly. He's a very good fellow, but at the beginning he believed that he had to play the habitual game in order to assert himself. Once he reached this understanding with me, the rules were different, we respected each other, and it was all for the better. And so, for me was "the good." But there was also "the bad."

Peter O'Toole?

Why, yes! In fact, the poor man was a wreck, destroyed by alcohol and drugs. The producer had forbidden him to arrive drunk for the first filming. So the first one went well; he was pretty much normal. But then, after the lights were set up, etc., he came back, and he was a different man, a zombie. I don't know what he took. In any case no communication was possible with him.

And Christopher Lee?

Ah, what an excellent actor! I'll tell you a story on this subject: He wore a wig. I knew it, but it was a secret, something sacred that could not be mentioned. Now, I wanted him to be bald in the film. They told me: "Impossible, you will never be able to get him to take off his wig." So I acted as if I didn't know that he wore a wig. I came to see him with a lady who took the measurements of his head in order to make him a bald cap.

When an actor has all his hair, but needs to appear bald on screen, a cap can be put on his head that gives the impression of baldness.

So we took his measurements and made the cap. And when he came to the filming, he had not put on the cap, but had simply taken off his wig! Everyone knew it, and he himself knew that we knew it, but no one said anything. It was nice, I had saved him from losing face by letting him do things the way he wanted, and he was content and very kind. A gentleman. One day I received a lesson from him relating to the law. We were in the middle of filming, it was four o'clock in the morning, and we still had to film two scenes: one in which there was an old man, ninety years old, and another with Christopher Lee. The technicians went to find the latter to ask him if they could begin by filming the scene with the old man, who was tired. Christopher Lee took a very clear position: "Things must not be done that way. It is absolutely prohibited. The law is clear: I am the actor, he is an extra; the law stipulates that I must be filmed first. If you do not respect the law, I will go and report it to the syndicate tomorrow." The technicians complied, and he was filmed first. I did not see this as the reaction of a cruel or egotistical being, but as the clear position of a man who does not accept it when people start bending the laws. One does not have the right to demand that someone else break the law.

Therefore, I received a lesson that day: there are legitimate demands and illegitimate demands. For example, when I read the tarot I am in the position of giving a gift. If someone comes to see me in this context and takes advantage of it by passing me his CV and asking me if I can recommend him as an actor to such and such a producer, that is not fair, and I do not have to tolerate it.

In this case, certainly, quite right. But the example of the old man appears to me a bit harsh. The technicians were acting out of kindness.

Indeed. But one must see the whole picture. The old man had agreed to be an extra, and his service was limited. After the filming of the scene, it was over. Christopher Lee was one of the three actors on whom the whole film depended. He still had a lot to do in the coming days and weeks; also, it would have created a precedent if he had accepted. The technicians would have had the impression that they could "string along" an actor at their convenience, rearranging things left and right. This may be a difficult example to understand for someone who is a total stranger to the world of film, but during a filming, there are laws that must be respected in order for all the people to stay in their proper places. Cases where it really is justified to take liberties with the law may exist, but they are rare. To respect the law is also to respect oneself.

After The Rainbow Thief, *did you not film anymore?*

No, but anything is possible. I receive a good number of offers. You know, I do not put any label on myself.

I do not identify as a film director. If there is a film to make, if things fall into place, then I make it; in that moment, because I am making it, I am the film director: that is my role. But then it's over until the next time, and I do not feel lost, nonexistent, if I am not filming. I do not identify as an author of "comics," a writer, someone who reads the tarot, or a therapist. I am all these things; they are different roles that I assume at the moment when I am playing them, but at the same time I do not identify myself with these roles.

You see, even today, just after meeting with you, I have a meeting here with a producer who is coming to see me to talk about a film project. So, who knows? If I do it, I do it, if I don't, I don't, that's all.

This makes me think of a joke. A man says: "My dog is perfectly obedient. The proof: I'll tell him either come here or don't, and he obeys me: he either comes or does not." Terrific, right? Ha ha ha! With life I am like the master with his dog: I am content with what happens and with what doesn't.

The film is made, the film is not made; I accept the will of life. You should understand, if I wish a priori for things to happen, I do everything in my power to make them happen. But what happens happens, ultimately, and all is well. I am mortal;

that's the way it is. I must accept that one day I will die. We must bow before what life wants.

Because we have been talking about the subjects of death and acceptance, I will permit myself to ask you an intimate and painful question. When we made La Tricherie sacrée, fifteen years ago, I often encountered one of your sons, Teo, a nice boy, full of life. Shortly afterward you lost him; life took him from you. Would you be willing to talk about how you got through this trial, without a doubt one of the most tragic that a human being can undergo: the loss of a child?

I learned a great deal from it. First there was enormous suffering. Even if you have understood many things and seen beyond appearances, this is the worst kind of suffering. My self was broken into a thousand pieces like a mirror. And it makes you feel like a plague victim, as if you had announced that you had a shameful illness. Then, with time, my self was reconstructed, piece by piece. There comes a moment when you feel strong again, but the pain never goes away. The human heart reacts like a vegetable: with animals the cells reproduce and a new skin appears where there was a wound; but if a tree has a hole in it, this hole remains until death. The only thing possible for the tree is to grow a new limb next to the place where it has lost one. Fungi may grow in the hole and nourish the tree, but the hole is never filled. Likewise, a pain like the one we speak of is never consoled. However, one may build many marvelous things next to it. This event taught me to live with pain. I know now that one can live with it, and I also know that love is stronger than pain. Love supports everything, it grows, and it lives in you at every moment. You know the episode where

Buddha advises a woman who has lost her son to go into all the houses in which no one has ever died. The death of a child is a tragedy for the parents, but it is also part of life. One of the great lessons that the death of a child teaches us is to be aware of the fact that we ourselves are mortal.

Then different lessons can come from death: you feel that the drop of water has returned to the ocean, that even if you are suffering, the dead no longer suffer.

Then comes the moment when you can rejoice at all that has been given to you, rather than crying over what you have lost; you feel gratitude for all the years shared with your child, instead of lamenting the years that will not be. Oh yes, you learn a lot of things, because you suffer, and it is from this suffering that your soul is born. What more can be said?

For six or seven years, I could not talk about it at all. I was in mourning. Today, I can talk about it.

And then something marvelous happened: When Teo died it was as if he had not left any trace. He was young and had not yet done anything significant. But six months later I learned that a woman was expecting a child by him, and today I am the grandfather of a little girl, his daughter, whom I love very much. And do you know what? She was conceived on the night of his death. He died by the side of the woman with whom he had just conceived a daughter. God takes away, God gives. Blessed be God.

We have just talked about a great misfortune. Alejandro, do you know ultimately whether happiness exists, and if so, what it is?

What is happiness? There are many definitions of it. According to the Germans happiness is doing work that pleases you. Why not? But if we want to take this further, I don't believe that one can grasp the concept of happiness other than through the negative: happiness is to be less anguished each day than the day before. What is strength? Being less weak every day than the day before. What is goodness? Doing less evil each day than the day before. And so on. These are pragmatic definitions, aren't they?

And you—what is happiness for you?

As for me, I can say that yes, I know happiness. You know, they asked Ramakrishna if he believed in God, and he answered: No, I do not believe in God because I know God. To know happiness is not a thought, but a sensation. As for me, I know happiness, I feel it. Of course I have my struggles, I suffer, and life deals me blows, like everyone else.

What's more, our society is sadistic; it tortures us in various ways. Despite all that, despite the death we have spoken about, I do feel the sensation of happiness and peace. It is there. It's not that I know it; I just feel it. The other day I saw a broadcast on the television where they were showing things like little transparent comets attacking the cells in the blood. What are those called?

Free radicals?

That's right, free radicals! Very bad, these free radicals, eh? Terrifying! It's stress. So I believe that when we are happy we also secrete little comets that go around inside us and prolong our lives. Happiness is the antistress.

Do great desires still reside within you?

You know, the other side of desire is fear. Animals spend their time being afraid; they are scared of being eaten. Animality *is* fear. The first step on the path of the spirit consists of putting fear back in its place. In the Bible, each time the angel appears, whether to Mary or Zechariah, he begins by saying, "Be not afraid."

As long as one is controlled by fear, one is not truly a human being. Society engenders a multitude of fears in order to keep us in an animal state and thus control us better. As for desire it is often nothing but the flip side, a compensation for this fear that inhabits us. Fundamentally the greatest and truest desire is the desire to be oneself. As one frees oneself little by little from animal fear and from the superficial desires that are only there to compensate for that fear, one ends up desiring nothing but that: to be oneself. As for me, my great desire today is to be myself. Now I already feel like myself! So what more can I desire, other than happy and positive things for those around me? I know that each person lives through his own trials and bears the cross that corresponds to him, which no one else can bear in his place.

PART THREE

Once There Was Jodo

Testimonies

What could be the common denominator between a great rock journalist, a former star of X-rated movies, a master of *bandes dessinées,* and the spiritual guide of an ashram? The answer: Jodorowsky, of course.

Without a doubt a whole book could be written about the "Jodorowsky galaxy" populated by the odd multitude of creative and remarkable people whose common factor is that they were all marked in one way or another—and often in many ways—by this remarkable man. Here one would find theater people, writers, psychiatrists, musicians, magicians, tarologists, spiritual teachers, illustrators, actors, filmmakers, experts in martial arts, prostitutes, and tax collectors.

As Jodo himself said to me: "Many people from different domains could testify to my influence on them, but you would do better to ask them to talk about it at my funeral."

Because, God forbid, it is not yet time to bury our friend, I have chosen the occasion of the "return" of *La Tricherie sacrée* to pick a representative handful of testimonies that may clarify and complete the perspective offered by our earlier and later conversations about a personality that decidedly defies categorization.

Philippe Manœuvre, Coralie Trinh Thi, François Boucq,

and Arnaud Desjardins all immediately and gladly seized this opportunity to pay a little of their tribute to Jodo. Each one took a very personal approach, very unlike the formulaic tone of "homage" that is often used when writing obligatory commendations.

When talking about Jodorowsky they each told a few stories, also sharing a small part of themselves. They showed an enthusiasm, an intelligence, and a sensitivity toward this totally unexpected man, whose depth and integrity had amazed them.

In addition to the testimonies of these four people, Jodorowsky had no hesitation in allowing me to include one of his three living sons, Adan. This audacity is noteworthy: what public figure would not tremble at seeing his statue rattled by the gaze of not only his friends, peers, and collaborators, but also those closest to him of all—the redoubtable test of intimacy?

Finally it seemed amusing to us to conclude this series of testimonies with a little Jodorowskian pirouette in which the roles are reversed, with the subject turning into the questioner, interrogating his interviewer, but still on the same subject: visits with Jodo.

SIX

THE GOOD DOCTOR OF ROCK

Interview with Philippe Manœuvre

Born in 1954 Philippe Manœuvre is undoubtedly the most famous French rock journalist (rock critic) still in action.

In addition to being a pillar of the heroic era of rock and folk, he has also been a pioneer of TV rock—via the magazine *Les Enfants du Rock,* the legendary TV show *Sex Machine* (hosted with Jean-Pierre Dionnet), and his appearances on the TV channels Canal+ and Jimmy.

He has met, interviewed, and been on tour with legendary figures ranging from the Rolling Stones to Iggy Pop, Lou Reed, James Brown, and members of the Beatles.

As editor in chief of the magazine *Métal Hurlant,* he has also made his mark on French *bandes dessinées.*

Philippe met with me in a large café near the Porte de Champerret, not far from his home. He is a very kind man, generous, and somewhat electric—in the sense of being supercharged, which is normal for someone involved in rock music. We discuss *Le Théâtre de la guérison* ("I am happy to meet you. I had wondered if you really existed or if you were a creation of Alejandro's"), and conclude with an homage to Jodo the Hero.

How did you meet Alejandro?

I met him at *Métal Hurlant*. I think it was after the *Dune* debacle. Alejandro had gathered around him a fabulous team to work on a project of adapting Frank Herbert's *Dune* for the screen. When it finally became clear that this film was not going to be made, the team scattered, and it was a bit of a tragedy. The *Dune* team actually did not want to break up, and a good part of the project's energy was reincarnated, so to speak, in *Métal Hurlant*. This was the time when Alejandro and Mœbius began collaborating on *bandes dessinées*. *Métal Hurlant* also was not lacking in colorful personalities. But all the same Alejandro was among the top three most, uh, hallucinatory characters.

How do you mean, hallucinatory? Tell me more about that.

Well, the first time I had breakfast with him, a girlfriend of mine was there with us, and he immediately explained to her how she had not been caressed enough when she was little. He told her incredible things about herself right away, like that. Then he showed her by massaging her. Nothing sexual, just proving it by touching her. Obviously, when things like that happen during a first breakfast together, you realize that you aren't dealing with an entirely ordinary person.

So we got along very well and saw each other often through *Métal Hurlant.*

Currently, what do you think of Jodo as a storyline writer for bandes dessinées?

I admire him a great deal. Storyline writers are not talked about enough. In this domain, as in many others, Alejandro rather defies categorization. He is not an ordinary storyline writer, someone who tells a story that Boucq, Mœbius, Bess, or someone else will put into images. He really gets his illustrators moving, makes them go further. More than a storyline writer, he's an initiator, he sends you on a voyage full of teachings. That's what it is to collaborate with Jodorowsky. In one way or another, one never leaves unchanged. He marks everyone he meets.

Was this the case for you during the Métal Hurlant period?

Yes, I was editor in chief of the magazine, but for me it was obvious that Alejandro was a master.

A master?

Yes, someone who knows things of which others are ignorant, who says things that no one else can say. A master, and how! With him one immediately enters into parallel universes. I remember one day he did a great tarot demonstration in the offices of the magazine. He had made a symbolic figure with the tarot cards in Dionnet's office, and people couldn't go in there.

He had arranged the cards in such a way that people could not even go into the room; a force kept them outside. That's the kind of thing he can do!

So, this is a personality around whom totally incredible things happen. Once he sent me a bottle of mescal from Mexico with a white worm at the bottom. It was a product that, at the time, could absolutely not be found in Europe. Beyond the bottle it was as if he had sent me something from another world, an unknown dimension.

Did you see him often?

Yes and no. At a *bandes dessinées* magazine, people don't come in every day, except at *Charlie Hebdo.* The magazine was somewhat at the mercy of the desires and adventures of each person. So we lost touch somewhat. And then I got back in touch with him years later.

Under what circumstances?

I don't remember; we saw each other again at *bandes dessinées* festivals. *Métal Hurlant* had been a great human and artistic adventure, an enterprise that left scars that marked all those who participated in it. So when we met again, we were a little like two old army pals. I had distanced myself from the *bandes dessinées* crowd because I had been disappointed with the attitude of many illustrators toward Jean-Pierre Dionnet when the problems with URSSAFF and other fun stuff happened. It was nothing too bad, but I felt distanced. And then I went to Mexico for the first time in my life. It was not too long ago; in the 1990s I went there to follow the AC/DC tour. Before leaving I called Alejandro to ask him what I should see and do down there, because he had lived there for a long time. And he gave me a secret mission.

A secret mission?

Yes, a personal one, for him. He needed certain things that had to be tracked down in areas of the city where the taxi drivers didn't want to go.

Did you carry out this mission?

Yes, I went there with an incredible escort! It seemed entirely incongruous to me. On the AC/DC tour, we were staying in a five-star hotel. In the hall there was a six-meter-high ice sculpture that was melting. It was sublime luxury.

When we had a day off between two concerts, I told the porter that I wanted to go to that area of the city. He replied, "Oh no, no one goes there, no way." I kept insisting; I wanted to keep my promise, and Alejandro had warned me that it would not be easy. So we went there. I accomplished the secret mission in that magical land.

With regard to Mexico and Alejandro, I must say that I have one regret: We spent one remarkable evening, during which Alejandro, surrounded by his sons, who were all there, told us about Mexican magic and the possibilities for discovery there. At the time I was a bit lazy, and I did not understand. I realize today that a documentary for Canal+ could have been made on this subject, starting with Alejandro talking about initiatory encounters in Mexico. We passed up an adventure.

So did you continue seeing each other?

I had done a service for him, he was pleased, and we began seeing each other more often. This was when the tarot began to interest me more. Because every time one sees Alejandro, he brings out his tarot cards.

Have you consulted him?

When I have a real problem, something that seems insurmountable to me, I don't go to a shrink, or to family members, or to a good friend; I go to consult Alejandro and his cards. This is my shock therapy. Every time he receives me very kindly. I have sometimes found myself in incredibly hard, difficult personal situations. When you go to see him in the midst of such a situation, Alejandro restores humor, kindness, and hope. He restores many essential things.

He conducted a therapy with me through the family tree at a time when I was at rock bottom. I was in the middle of a divorce, a hard, ruthless divorce. Alejandro led me to take a new view of this woman whom I was in the process of divorcing, showing me that we had been the victims of a very rare case: if you superimposed my wife's family tree upon my own, you could see that they were the same! We were like brother and sister. Everything had gone very well when we were just living together, but from the day that we got married, we had fallen into a terrifying abyss. Alejandro picked apart the mechanisms of this for me, and this helped me to gain a little bit of distance, to see this person, who had become my enemy, in a different way. He also warned me against the tarots of Aleister Crowley. Someone had recommended them to me, and Alejandro said: "Throw those away immediately; otherwise you will attract very real, terrible forces." Not all tarot decks are good; this is what he taught me. At that time we also compared our readings of Éliphas Levi, which was fabulous.

So you benefited from Alejandro's availability.

That's one of his characteristics: his amazing availability! I have sent people to him several times, and he has always received them with great generosity, a great deal of openness, kindness, and also honesty. When he has the impression that he can do nothing more, he says so clearly. Yes, he has helped all of us very much.

By "all of us" do you mean the milieus of bandes dessinées and rock music?

Yes, that network, among others. It's true that Alejandro is a rock guru, one of those rare people who is recognized both as an artist and as a spiritual reference for many rock stars. All the same John Lennon called him "master." The Beatles were enthralled with him, and they produced several of his films.

Unfortunately, as those familiar with the band's history know, their manager Allen Klein swindled them terribly and restricted the rights to many of their undertakings, including certain films by Jodorowsky. Alejandro also found himself a prisoner of this sinister character. He brought Alejandro checks offered by the Beatles for several films to be made, but in exchange Klein became producer, keeping the rights, controlling everything.

Alejandro has met many brilliant people in his life, but he has also dealt with shadows.

Yes, this Mr. Klein, about whom Lennon wrote the song "Steel and Glass"; his web extended over all of English rock during the 1960s.

A shadow, and not a small one.

A shadow cast over the Beatles, the Stones, and over Jodorowsky.

So, Alejandro has been, and still is, a rock guru. Discretion obliges me not to mention many names, but I do know that numerous musicians admire him and consult him. This ranges from very young rockers to great prestigious names, such as Peter Gabriel, whom I can mention because he himself has spoken about Alejandro.

One may also mention Marilyn Manson. A story on this subject: One must know that when one is with Alejandro, the coincidences pile up in a totally incredible manner. It's a mysterious phenomenon that one can only observe and that takes place unceasingly. One day, when I had not spoken with Alejandro for a year, I was at a hotel in London to do an interview there with Marilyn Manson.

While I was in the elevator with this latter, my mobile phone rang, and it was Alejandro, asking me if I had the telephone number of . . . Marilyn Manson! To which I answered: "No, but I can pass you right over to him." This kind of thing happens all the time with Alejandro.

I greatly enjoy taking him to concerts from time to time. He still wants to go to rock concerts, which is admirable at his age, given the fatigue this sort of event can bring about— one must often stand amid a frenetic crowd until late into the night. He loves it; he loves rock; he loves the release of energy.

In my view the world of rock needs more people like him, able to take a different, broader view of all this madness, able to put it all in perspective.

What is he to you today? A master, a therapist, a friend? All these things at once?

It's a bit of a father-son relationship, by reason of our ages, because he is exactly the same age as my real father. A father is always there in hard times.

It's very comforting to know that if I have a true, serious problem, I can go to see Alejandro. I just used the term "rock guru," but I must explain that Alejandro has never wanted to be a guru in the negative sense of the term. He has never sought to found a sect or a group devoted to him, even if that might have been fairly easy. He has never wanted to make people pay, which is quite incredible for our era! In him we see a phenomenon that is in the process of vanishing: a disinterested person and true goodness. We need more people like him on this Earth.

SEVEN

THE ARCHETYPE OF
THE FATHER
Interview with
Coralie Trinh Thi

Coralie Trinh Thi, born in 1976, received the prestigious Hot d'Or award in 1996 and 1998 and in 1995 the award for best French X-rated film actress. At the beginning of the twenty-first century, she went behind the camera and codirected the film *Baise-moi* with Virginie Despentes. She contributed to *Rock & Folk* and in 2002 published her first novel, *Betty Monde* (Au Diable Vauvert).

Although the famous film left me perplexed—I did watch it quickly—her novel made a strong impression on me, with its clashing of magic, spiritual quests, sex, drugs, and rock and roll, all interspersed with very insightful reflections on child-hood, compassion, and the wounds of the soul. This book is at once raw and subtle, far removed from the flood of insipid soup served up year after year under the label "novel." Thus, I had the feeling of already knowing her a little when, in 2003, I opened the door of my home in Paris to a young woman with whom a dialogue immediately began that went much farther than the inherently artificial exercise known as an interview. She is very much like her book and has been very successful, considering she is only twenty-seven years old. If I had to choose a few adjectives to describe my impression of Coralie, I would say: present, rational, precise, exacting, and . . . modest. Not exactly one's preconceived notion of a former X-rated movie actress, and so much the better! Any lingering prejudice vaguely floating in my consciousness was immediately destroyed.

When and how did you meet Alejandro?

The meeting occurred after the debut of the film I codirected with Virginie Despentes, *Baise-moi*.

Baise-moi was made during a particular period of my life when I had deadened my emotions with coke in order to speed up my head, because I felt that I was under incredible pressure, which, it seemed impossible for me to survive by normal means. I was entirely conscious of what I was doing when I was getting high on cocaine, going "berserk" as they say, giving enormous power to the mental faculties. The problem was that when I stopped using coke, I didn't come back down! I remained completely cut off from my emotions, from my body, from myself. I was seized by general nihilism à la Nietzsche, but much darker! It was like a dead-end street. I did not know how to go any further with my intellect, and it took me absolutely nowhere. I was lost, and this must have shown. So much so that Philippe Manœuvre, whom I had met, thanks to an article about *Baise-moi,* suggested to me out of kindness that I should meet Jodorowsky. I had absolutely no idea who he was talking about, and Philippe was very surprised by this, considering Jodo's great fame as a *bandes dessinées* storyline writer. In short I didn't know about Jodorowsky, and what's more I couldn't care less! However, Philippe Manœuvre had so much respect and admiration for him, he had the air of giving me an enormous gift in arranging a private meeting with this man, and it seemed tactless to refuse. So I accepted, very halfheartedly, without any faith at all. I was sure that no one could help me. Philippe Manœuvre just mentioned to me that he had told Jodorowsky that I had "lost my center," and this expression really hit home with me, so much so that I had a slight change of mood as I set out to meet with him.

I remember it was December 22, 2000. Jodorowsky was very cautious with me. He sat me down near a window and began to reassure me a great deal about lots of things that had not bothered me at all. He manifested immense benevolence. For my part I tested him a lot, a bit like a kid who wants to have confidence but can't have all that much, and he reacted really well, without getting annoyed at any point.

How did you test him?

By contradicting him, by trying to verify his expertise and the understanding he might have of a problem. It's difficult to describe without recounting the entire conversation in detail, but yes, I really tested him. What made the greatest impression on me was that he entirely understood what I was doing and never took offense. From beginning to end he remained absolutely sure of himself. I believe that in his place I would have quickly become annoyed, but he didn't even flinch.

From there he drew my family tree for me and asked me to formulate three wishes. Strangely I had a lot of trouble. I realized that I did not know what I wanted, or didn't want to say it, or even was not ready to say it to myself! Ultimately this realization was the most important element of that first conversation.

That being said I was still required to make three wishes. I did not express the thing that was most important to me—heartache; I formulated a wish for my novel—*Betty Monde,* which has since been written and published by Diable Vauvert—which I had not yet written at the time, even though I had all the elements in place. I couldn't get to work on it! So he prescribed a psychomagical act for me for writing this novel, which I was able to carry out soon after departing. I also expressed the wish to cut painful ties with certain people in my family; for this, also, he prescribed an act for me.

Finally, instead of talking about my heartache with him, I told him that I wanted to move to a new home—which, without doubt, was fundamental to that period.

Did you carry out the prescribed acts?

Something interesting happened: I wanted to begin with the act that was intended to allow me to cut certain ties. I began it, but did not carry it through. I tried again, but again I didn't complete it. I dragged it out for a long time, until I finally realized that in fact, this was not what I really wanted! How can I describe this act? I told Jodorowsky that I felt like I was dragging around a ball and chain. He gave me an object that resembled a cannonball, and told me to write the names of the people in question on it, then to carry it around in my bag in order to feel its weight, then throw it into the Seine as soon as I felt that I'd had enough of it. But I never performed this last step. There were two names: one has naturally worn off, and the tie with this person has broken of its own accord; as for the other I came to realize that I did not want to sever the connection any longer, and there was still some work on this relationship that remained for me to do.

So, what did you do?

The thing that represented the cannonball was, in fact, a work of art. Instead of throwing it away, I put it on a shelf, in a nice spot, next to my Hot d'Or award.

Ultimately, would you say that the act worked?

It was even more effective than anticipated. Each time Jodo prescribed a magical act, even if it seemed to be far out or not really what you wanted, you would still end up resolving something.

And for your book?

I don't want to reveal the prescribed act. Let's just say that I followed his instructions precisely and that it worked. Note that at the beginning I thought he was completely off the mark. So at first I didn't do it, but since I was still not writing, I finally decided to carry out the act, long afterward, in February 2002. Before doing it I was terrified. I had to confront my fear in order to begin.

Finally I carried out the magical act according to his instructions, then did it a second time, modifying it in a way that, without my knowing it, presaged the ending of my novel. Writing this book was in itself a magical act, a process of individualization that allowed me to work through things. Alejandro certainly played a decisive role in this process.

And the third act?

Its purpose was for me to be able to move. I moved to Brittany, where I took a training course, and when I returned to Paris, I found a letter from my landlord terminating my lease! It was as if the act had caused a miracle of synchronicity. I was obliged to move.

There are the acts themselves, then their effects; beyond the acts there is also the impact that the meeting with Jodo had on you. Philippe Manœuvre told him that you had "lost your center." Did you rediscover it after this contact?

What really helped me is that it reintroduced magic into my life. I remember listening to him describe the acts to me and saying to myself: "But I know all this already!"

I had practiced magic earlier, and his intervention made me realize that I had obscured a part of myself, had forgotten all about magic and spirituality, even though I had placed a great deal of importance in these things during my "goth" period. I had specialized in self-enchantment, but without knowing about Alejandro's method. I don't mean by this that I was invoking demons or spirits, but that I was using the power of symbols to condition myself, in a positive sense, to act on will. So I was performing psychomagic without knowing it.

You used the word "spiritual"; magic and spirituality are not synonymous.

Of course not, but envisaging "magic" in a certain way, as a use of symbols and archetypes, leads one to discover traditional cosmogonies, such as those that were rediscovered and used from a psychoanalytic perspective by Jung. Personally, I do not believe that people have contact with the spirits of the dead or with any sort of demons. For me the approach known as magic is a tool for accessing one's subconscious.

I agree. So this is where you coincide with Jodorowsky in his psychomagical approach, which consists of programming the subconscious, as it were, by means of an act.

Exactly. I have never approached magic as a way of having power over others, but as a technique for working on oneself.

And Jodorowsky reintroduced this dimension into your life?

That's right. I had a profound need to reconnect with this part of myself. It was like rediscovering my path, a direction in which to go, but without being certain of what was at the end. This encounter truly repaired something. I was dead inside, and he breathed life back into me.

Did you continue to see him afterward?

Yes, I went to see him for tarot readings. As you know he reads the tarot regularly, for free, at a café in Paris; so I watched him at work, and I learned more from that than from anything else ever. When he reads the cards, he is absolutely not an ordinary man.

What do you mean?

I mean that he is "in a state of holiness." When I tell him this, it annoys him; he thinks I am denying his human aspect. But no, what I mean is that he is in a state of grace. I have often sat beside him during his readings and seen people physically change at the moment when they sit down in front of him. It's as if their masks are pulled back, and you can read what's inside them. Perhaps Jodo can already read what's inside them before the mask is pulled back, I don't know. In any case you know what they are going to say before they begin to speak. It's very impressive. In this way I have witnessed some small miracles.

For example?

Well, I don't know whether there is sometimes "sacred trickery" . . .

Jodo seems to have intuitions, to know what card is underneath. I'd like to believe that perhaps he can sometimes even see through it. But not always. He will say to the person, "you will draw such and such a card." Then that happens, and as far as I can see, Jodo has no rational way of predicting it. When he prescribes psychomagical acts, he appears to be profoundly inspired. But what makes the greatest impression on me, and what I have learned the most from, is that he is in a state of non-judgment. If I were to say that he is in a state of absolute love, that would risk being misinterpreted. What I mean is that in that moment his gaze is on a different plane: at once extremely lucid—he truly sees through people—and devoid of all judgment. It may sound stupid to say it in this way, but it seems to me that this kind of viewpoint is one of the most difficult things to attain in life: to be capable of seeing all sorts of things in other people, but without judging them at all. One has to be extremely strong! So, yes, seeing him able to do this for people has overwhelmed me.

Can you explain further? How do you mean, overwhelmed?

It's not like "When I grow up I want to be like Jodorowsky"—I don't want to be Jodorowsky; I want to be myself. It's more about possibilities for personal development. Jodo seems to me to have reached, as a person, a level of consciousness that makes me envious, inspires me, and not only in the realm of the tarot. Here I am talking about the therapist, not the everyday human, about whom I ultimately know very little. It's like the same person in two different roles. And Jodo the therapist, who welcomes people and helps to heal them in a disinterested way, shows me a field of possible evolution. Indeed, I believe that the human being is made for traversing many crises, each one of which causes him to grow. So the concept of "level of consciousness" can be rather vague, and it's as if Jodo, through who he is, showed me what is right and showed me how to continue progressing on this plane. This is not meant to place Jodorowsky on some pedestal, at the top of humanity or wherever. But he is the first person I have met whose level of consciousness really made an impression on me.

This level of consciousness seems to me inseparable from an aptitude for benevolence and non-judgment.

Through him you have seen how a human being can be tuned in to another wavelength.

Yes, in this moment he is truly different. I suppose that when he is making a film, he is also different, likewise when he is writing. He has many sides, but this particular side is incredibly luminous.

Today how would you describe your relationship with him?

To answer this I will return to my novel, *Betty Monde*. You observed that this book is dedicated to him—the dedication is at the end ("To Alejandro Jodorowsky, thank you . . ."). The first word of the book is a dedication to Willy, my father: "To Willy, for the Lead." In fact, it's an alchemical dedication. So the first word of the book is a dedication to my father, and the last word of the book is a thanks to Jodorowsky. It was not planned; I only realized it after the fact: I realized that in this book I do an enormous amount of work with the image of man, and therefore, inevitably, that of the father. Now, I am not sure that I would have been able to repair the image of the father if I had not met Jodorowsky. Not that I consider any man worthless, but in terms of my personal history, this is the only male image that I totally respect. In fact, respect is not the right word; I can respect people without being fundamentally impressed by them. So it's not exactly respect. One can respect a child, for example, but this does not make the child into a fundamental image. So what would be the right word? Help me; you know how to work with words!

Is it a matter of confidence? In his presence you felt a man who was strong, structured, and therefore reassuring, completely a man, but one who was not going to abuse his strength, his authority, or the influence he might have had over you.

Yes, it's true. This is an extremely important point in my relationship with Jodorowsky. I know that he will never abuse the ascendancy that people give to him. I believe that he is entirely aware of his power, and consequently his responsibility, when he reads the tarot in a café, for example. It is said that the shaman is fueled by the faith his patients have in him. Likewise, I believe that Alejandro is fully conscious of this power and will never abuse it, neither on me nor on anybody else.

I have never felt or suspected that he has a "guru" side to him, in the bad sense of the term, which many therapists can have. I say "guru" in the bad sense because it seems that this word has acquired a thoroughly different meaning.

A guru in the original sense of the term is someone who bears great wisdom, great maturity. He is an instructor, and above all, a disciple, a servant. He can therefore lead an ashram, a community, or accompany people on their path of development and bear witness to a level of consciousness that is higher than the ordinary—but always in service to others, not serving himself.

Well, in this case he is far from what "guru" has come to mean in our vocabulary, namely the leader of a sect who makes others stupid and infantile by playing on his own charisma. I do not condone this. For me this is precisely the proof that someone has not surpassed his own ego, and that is completely pathetic. Now, I have never felt this with Jodorowsky. Therefore, I have confidence in him, but this is not blind confidence. I do not believe that he knows better than me about what is good for me; instead I feel that he can help me to discover myself. This is what I call a master or a guide: someone who helps others to become themselves.

Traditionally it is said that the guru is nothing other than yourself, further along your own path.

Yes, without a doubt. When I just said "when I grow up I want to be like Jodorowsky," it was a joke, but it was also a way of saying that later I would like to attain this level, to be capable of helping people in this way. Of course, this will first require that I heal personally from many things. But I have very often found myself in the situation of helping people, even though lacking the tools to do so. Jodo has also helped me in this regard. Once, notably, I did something foolish with the tarot.

What was this foolish thing?

Not really foolish, but I do not have the level of consciousness necessary for understanding my reading of the tarot. Even if I had understood, I would have been in big trouble, because this was not something that could be resolved in this way. He helped me to rectify the mistake.

Another paternal function: the father who helps one to become oneself and sometimes helps to rectify errors.

For sure. Because you have read my novel, you have read the passages where Betty Monde talks about her father. That is my story.

This reminds me of the following beautiful passage:

> Her father died of an overdose when she was a child. Obviously, they tried to protect her by concealing the shameful death. Or perhaps they were trying to protect her from herself, because adults believe that what is unsaid is non-existent. They do not know that blushing, pale, or tense bodies, averted or troubled eyes, silences and breaths, speak to those who know how to observe. All children know. The

difference is that the child must search within herself for the courage to lean out, all alone, into the abyss that she perceives. She must confront and conquer her guilt: How could I imagine that people were lying to me, why would I deserve to be lied to? And the fear of being dragged down by adults, who turn their backs to the abyss. Upon reflection, Betty is not sure that the word "adult" is the most appropriate when speaking of family secrets.

What I did not put in the novel is that it appears to have been a suicide and not an accident with the drug. He had kicked the habit, it was very hard, and his mother had died shortly beforehand.

It was in 1982, I was six years old, and I only really learned about his death when I was eleven or twelve. This is why I call family secrets a crime.

When adults concentrate on not saying something, what children pick up on is a kind of retention, a mask.

So I quickly understood that I was working on my relationship with men and with my father. Therefore, I found a magical super-act for myself that consisted of burning my book on my father's grave. I was very happy with my idea and did not at all realize that it was symbolically negative and shabby. Once the book was finished, I found myself unable to let go of the manuscript to have it published; it was a truly terrible crisis. I was sure that I was going to commit suicide, to the point that I did not dare to get out of bed, because I was convinced that if I passed the window I would jump out! This is funny to me now, but at the time I was prey to a morbid compulsion that I had never before confronted. Sure, we all cry and sometimes tell ourselves we're going to die, but it had never happened to me before in this form and to such a degree. It was terrifying, as if I were dealing with a will that was not my own. I got through the whole night by telling myself that I was going to call Jodo—I absolutely did not want to call him at one in the morning! So I called him the next day. He talked to me for a long time. In fact, he began by going into what I call his "trance." I think that he remembers my call but not all the details. I suddenly realized how sleazy my magical act was! I also looked at my tattoo [*Coralie shows me a tattoo on her arm*]—these are runes. Here, this was supposed to be the sun, but I got it wrong: it looks a little like the sun, but in fact it's death! I committed a sort of Freudian slip in designing this tattoo, because I knew the runes very well: I changed the symbol of the sun, which is eminently paternal, into the symbol of death. What a stupid act! I realized all this at the same time and was completely terrified. Fortunately, this is not the last tattoo, after it comes the symbol of plenty. Jodo explained to me that I was possessed by the spirit of my father, not in the literal sense, but psychologically. He ended up adopting me spiritually. But note: this is nothing like what it might appear to be superficially. What I mean is that many people look for a father figure in him, want to spend time with him, want him to pay attention to them, and so on. This "adoption" was not at all on an ordinary plane of reality, but in the archetypal dimension. At the moment when I needed it, he incarnated the archetype of the father for me, made me feel that he would never abandon me and would not die. He was the only person I could allow to incarnate this archetype for me.

So you gave up the idea of burning your book on your father's grave.

Fortunately! On the contrary Jodorowsky told me to bring him an advance copy as soon as I could. I had not considered it at the time, but I realized later that this was something I profoundly needed and that it related to my half-baked idea of a magical act.

This adoption was a daring move on his part, even on the archetypal plane.

I think—perhaps I am totally wrong, but this is what I believe today—that he felt authorized to do it because he felt that I would not get the levels mixed up. I was aware that this adoption took place on another level of reality. He knows that I'm a big girl, that I won't start bothering him and calling him every day.

That you won't ask him to be your father.

Exactly! He knows that this act has no significant consequences on daily life. He has dealt with delicate situations before. He has girls who come to his tarot meetings with unreasonable demands for him, they cry, and it is not his role to respond to this thirst for love. He also has all the people who are searching for a master without knowing how to express themselves clearly, and he often sends them to Arnaud Desjardins. In short, he knew that I was not going to confuse symbolic adoption with legal adoption. I have plenty more of my path to follow, and I will meet other totally fabulous people. But at the moment when I met him, he was really the only person capable of doing this for me.

I want to add one more thing: it was very important to me that Jodo had a companion, and a companion whom I could also admire. Things would undoubtedly have been less simple had this not been the case. Marianne is an admirable being, and the fact that he has a good emotional life with her counts for a great deal—even if he has two aspects in himself, masculine and feminine. It reassures me a great deal to see this man, who has attained a level of consciousness very superior to mine, capable of living in a healthy and enriching relationship.

Today, at a little more distance, what place does he hold for you?

There are two distinct things: as the person who repaired my paternal archetype, as he himself has said, nothing would change, even if I never saw him again or if he died. It is done, and cannot be undone. Otherwise we are friends. I do not see him very often, but it is always a pleasure; we share news regularly and have dinner along with other people.

I also sometimes ask him for esoteric direction and for advice. For example, at the moment I am involved somewhat in alchemy, in relation to a book I want to write about my X-rated experiences; now, he has such an original esoteric vision, he is like a slightly mad artist. In his approach to healing, Jodo is completely an artist, with an enormous amount of intuition, with qualities of genius. He is someone completely incredible. Once again, Alejandro Jodorowsky, thank you.

EIGHT

THE DELIVERER FROM WORLD TO WORLD
Interview with
François Boucq

Born in 1955 François Boucq has published over twenty-five albums; he is considered one of the masters of contemporary francophone *bandes dessinées*. He received the Alfred award for best album in 1986 for *La femme du magicien* (cowritten with Jérôme Charyn), the prize for best BD album at Charleroi, and the RTL prize for BD in 1991. In 1998 he was awarded the Angoulême Grand Prize for all of his work in the *bandes dessinées* realm.

I had a few memories of brief encounters with François Boucq in Vincennes. This time we met at his home in Lille, where he was born and always lived, and where I went to seek him out the day after Christmas. I discovered a welcoming man, very serene and attentive to others. He gave me a tour of his city, showing me the superb arches built in the city center by his friend Jean-Claude Meizières. Boucq himself designed a fountain for the city, which forms part of the new face of this place where history and modernity are magnificently united. Our interview took place at an Italian restaurant in the old quarter, Place aux Oignons, where he is a regular.

The menu even included a "François Boucq Platter," which I could not resist trying: a dish that was succulent but subtle, much like its namesake. An advanced practitioner of kendo (I learned that he has been to Japan many times to train with old masters in the traditional dojos), Boucq takes care to preserve the lucidity that is essential for his creations and does not drink or eat copiously in the middle of the day. He is not a monk, but a disciplined artist, concentrating on what is essential.

After the interview we met with a group of old friends and spent a convivial day after Christmas. We joked about Jodorowsky's curious "handicap" whereby he views every trip as a big expedition. "Good thing Marianne buys his tickets and organizes everything, or else he would hardly be able to find the Gare du Nord. . . ." It is a strange side to an artist who has become internationally known and who, in fact, has traveled a great deal. I told François about the day in Vincennes when Jodo, in the midst of making contacts to film *The Rainbow Thief,* told me, thoroughly annoyed: "I am going to London to meet with a producer. In Piccadilly . . . where is this place, Piccadilly?"

"But Alejandro, it's a bit like if you asked me where Bastille Square is."

"Ah, I can't find the piece of paper, too bad."

Then, rummaging through a pile of papers, he pulled out an address: "Ah, there it is, now I can go there!"

After Boucq did a drawing for me on the flyleaf of *Bouncer*, volume III, I autographed my *Manuel de l'Anti-sagesse* for him, with a little drawing of a devil with horns and a pitchfork, as I usually do. He then began an impressive therapeutic interpretation of my scribbling: he kindly identified various aspects of my personality that were entirely legible to him through my childish drawing, rather like an astrologer looking at my horoscope. I was then better able to understand what he means by the therapeutic use of drawing.

Later, accompanying me to the train station, he told me about how he had tried the same experiment with various residents of Lille and told me of his idea for a television show on which people would simply be asked to draw something in front of the camera. Who knows what this might reveal? For example, what if our politicians were to do this—if they would agree to participate?

On his way out of the Italian restaurant, he told the managers about his participation, for the feast of Epiphany, in a project of the Ludopital Association, the goal of which is to improve the experience of children who are hospitalized. The cook would make galettes, and Boucq would decorate. In short Boucq is a passionate and generous man with many tricks up his sleeve.

Under what circumstances did you meet Jodorowsky?

Professional circumstances. We met about a year and a half before the release of the first album we did together, *Face de Lune—La Cathédrale invisible*. So it was in the late 1980s. Jean Annestay, who was working at Casterman on *À Suivre* at the time, said to me: "You know, Alejandro Jodorowsky might be interested in working with you." I said, "Ah yes, why not?"

and he set up a meeting with Jodo. The story of our first meeting is a little strange in itself. We set a date, and at the time it was not one hour but two hours by train from Lille to Paris. Consequently, if we wanted to have enough time to get to know each other and think up some projects, it was necessary to dedicate a whole day to it. So I bought my ticket and booked a hotel in Paris. At the last minute Alejandro told me he couldn't make it. Okay, this was no big deal. We could set another date; I changed my ticket and my hotel reservation. And the same scenario—last-minute cancellation by Jodorowsky—happened three or four more times!

Well, I did not know Alejandro, and the fourth time I said to Jean Annestay, who had organized the meeting: "Listen, after all this, if he wants to meet me, let's meet halfway." So we arranged to meet in Amiens. This time the interview was not canceled. We met at the cathedral steps and went out to eat together.

Rather symbolic, isn't it? At the cathedral steps. Your first album would be called La Cathédrale invisible.

Absolutely! I remember the first thing he said to me: "Well, Boucq, is your ego satisfied? Jodorowsky has come to you!" We began to discuss interesting things that we might be able to develop in the realm of *bandes dessinées,* and we soon agreed on the idea of building a cathedral. We said: "No one builds cathedrals anymore; why don't we build a new one in a BD?" Then we went into the cathedral of Amiens, which has remained a fundamental element in the series we conceived. We also walked the labyrinth together and got an idea of the initial basis for the story.

Is it true that at the time you shared Jodorowsky's interest in the symbols of esotericism?

To a certain extent, yes. From the beginning the circumstances of our meeting were not fortuitous. I have said that he wanted to work with me, but I had also been very interested in meeting him. I really liked *The Incal, The White Llama,* and I had seen *El Topo* in the cinema when I was a kid—I must have been seventeen. For me Jodorowsky represented an intriguing character and an intriguing artistic world. Intriguing because he was an artist in whom I could see an aspiration to another, more vast dimension. This intrigued me because, more or less vaguely, I was interested in all this.

At the time I had already begun an exploration with Father Jean Betous, an old canon who was passionate about the Golden Number. Once, at Christmastime, this man presented me with a deck of cards. I wondered why he gave me such a gift. Now, these were tarot cards, a deck that was missing all the major arcana. Fifteen days later I met Jodorowsky, who explained it to me and showed me the missing ones! I saw this as a sort of sign and had no hesitation in throwing myself into the adventure of *La Cathédrale invisible.* I was able to articulate what I had learned about the "divine proportion" with Alejandro's wildly artistic side. When I say "wild" I certainly do not mean random. Jodorowsky's "wildness" is rooted in very powerful symbolic knowledge.

Jodorowsky quickly became a sort of mentor for you, an initiator, as he had also been, I believe, in his relationship with Mœbius.

Yes and no, because from the beginning he set things up on

the artistic level. He told me: "Okay, we will make a creation together. We each know things about cathedrals, but we will not try to make an erudite album that will explain their esotericism. We will produce a work that is totally poetic." We then began our adventure in the form of a discussion. This is how things take place between us: we discuss; then he takes charge of the elements of the discussion to make the storyline from it. In terms of the creative process, he has a few anxieties about me, because I have a reputation for quarreling with my storyline writers. I quarreled with Jérôme Charyn, with whom I made two albums. Alejandro, who was aware of this, immediately tried to forestall any possible quarrels—which, in fact, have never happened.

So all that took place between him and me occurred in the course of the artistic process, without there being any need for formalities such as "teaching."

I remember the first time that I asked him, "ultimately, what is tarot?" He spent an hour explaining to me simply what was in one single card, just so that I could get an idea of it. At that time I thought I understood in principle how a sword in tarot should be viewed. Then he allowed me to sit with him while he read cards at the café in Paris. This made me eager to understand everything one could see through an image—I, whose work consisted of making images, to become conscious of what one can read in them—and at the same time what one can put into them.

But what I want to make clear in response to your question is that even these very seminal moments with regard to the tarot occurred naturally, as the natural outcome of our artistic collaboration. It was not a context of formal teaching, but of empathy in which many things took place.

Sometimes I almost had the feeling that I was going to see him in order to receive these little nuggets that he was giving me quite voluntarily, but conveyed in this way, underhandedly.

I enjoyed this greatly, because it is a method that keeps things free. And in any case I was never looking for a master-student relationship with him, because we were not positioned a priori on this level. On the contrary I learned from him, and learned a great deal, simply by being and working with him.

So, would you say that Jodorowsky does not have the urge to teach?

Not with me, in any case. Infusion seems the best description.

With time did this relationship mature?

Inevitably. It ripened. I also happily participated in many events in his life: joyous moments, painful moments. The ties of sympathy and friendship were reinforced over the years, along with the artistic relationship. Collaboration on this level grew closer and closer.

You insist, naturally, on the artistic dimension; can you say a little about the manner in which you perceive Jodorowsky as an artist?

What fascinates me about him is his artistic openness. It is rare to see someone with such a wealth of artistic inventiveness. What's more, it's a contagious wealth. I mean that he gives me the possibility of thinking of myself differently as an artist; he leads me to broaden my perception of myself. In my experience this is one of the very striking things that result from contact from him: he leads you to feel less and less limited in your artistic conception. But never by trying to dominate your creation, never by trying to make his approach prevail over yours: he does it by testifying, by demonstrating his own artistic experience, which is an experience of freedom and constant broadening. In contact with such energy, the result is that you give yourself the means for broadening your own conception. This stops you from getting frozen in a monolithic view of your practice. That is marvelous. Through his experience he allows you to better formulate things you were able to conceive intuitively, but unable to allow yourself even to think. Artistic freedom initially comes from the permission one gives oneself to create something. Jodorowsky, in his creation, allows himself to think differently, and his example leads you to say: "Why not me?"

For example?

Let's take the idea of artistic practice as therapy: it's something I had envisaged in a confused way, without being capable of clarifying it. He allowed me to begin to truly comprehend it.

You have just mentioned this freedom that Jodorowsky reveals in creation. Just before, you mentioned having been close to him as a friend during various moments in his existence. Have you found this freedom to be present in his way of living, of facing challenges?

Completely, and sometimes in a surprising manner. You know he has lost a son; when this tragedy occurred we were in the process of writing the last chapters of *Face de Lune, la Pierre de Faîte*. I saw how he kept working in the midst of all the emotional burdens associated with this drama. He never excluded anything in his manner of confronting all the dimensions of the emotional suffering this caused. I saw how he accepted the situation for what it was and penetrated into all its aspects, trying not to obliterate anything. I do not believe he is detached from this suffering today.

We talked about it in the new dialogues.

In any case this allowed him to know himself better in this dimension, to understand better how suffering operates on the heart in such a tragic experience, and also how it can come to imprison one's consciousness. Being equipped with strategies to deal with pain allows one to alleviate it and to avoid being trapped for life by such a cruel event. This is also why I love Alejandro: the ability he always has to draw the lesson out of an experience, however unbearable it may be, to draw an acute and pointed lucidity out of it, and to have the courage to hide nothing. He goes through to the end without protecting himself, without deciding: "No, this aspect is too painful, I cannot face it."

So, you have seen him "practice what he preaches"—even if in this case "preach" is not the proper word; you have seen that he embodies what he transmits in his creation.

Exactly, and this is what I appreciate about him: he's someone who measures up to what he says. He translates what he says into his everyday experience, and also uses this experience to enrich his perception.

There is an integrity about him that causes me to count him among those few persons whom I can describe as exemplary.

All the people I have asked to talk about him have insisted on his goodness. Ultimately, this is rather rare today. They praise his artistic genius as a remarkable creator, his boldness, and perhaps his kindness, sometimes. But in Jodo's case the words "goodness" and "generosity" keep cropping up every time. Are these the qualities that you also would emphasize?

You know, when someone decides to spend one afternoon per week doing something for free, and keeps it up for years, decades in fact—how long has he been reading cards at the café, hosting the "Mystic Cabaret"?

He was already doing it when I first met him fifteen years ago.

Well, then—such acts say far more than words.

I am also very much convinced of Alejandro's goodness, and I know that if we continue we will go in the direction of hagiography. So tell me, have you also seen the sides of him that are, let's say, more ordinary?

Of course, I have seen him get angry; I have seen his human sides. But that is good too! He is not someone ethereal who exudes excessive or effusive goodness. He is who he is, including what one might call his faults—who doesn't have faults?—and it seems to me that he accepts himself exactly as he is. He always has this attitude, toward others, toward life, toward himself: "Okay, there is this thing, this manifestation, this is how it is: what's the reality underneath it all?" He practices the benevolent exploration of the human being, beginning with himself. He sometimes says to me: "You know, I enjoy imitating holiness."

Yes, I believe I remember him saying this in La Tricherie sacrée. *In fact, "imitation" is a very noble spiritual concept. A famous mystical book of Christianity is titled* The Imitation of Christ; *more relevant to us, I am also reminded of a saying by Lee Lozowick: "Fake it till you make it."*

That's good, isn't it? Why not also imitate goodness, which, furthermore, is not incompatible with anger? Anger traverses individuals and can sometimes be a voluntary act. Demonstrating goodness is not so easy. Sometimes, despite all arguments against it, being good requires one to manifest a certain amount of anger.

In this case it's a question of knowing why this anger is there and at what it is directed, at what moment. I have seen Alejandro show goodness, I've seen him show anger, I've seen him in all the dimensions of the human being, and ultimately I would say that none of these dimensions monopolizes my attention any more than any other.

He expresses a whole range of possibilities, but always with a conscious will to explore and teach in the background. I would like to add something else. We have talked about goodness and generosity. I find that with Alejandro there is a dimension that is more and more rare, less and less often encountered: that of empathy. Empathy is a relational quality that is partly made up of precaution: being aware that the other person is not a homunculus within our own world; remembering that in the presence of another person, I am looking at a world as rich and complete as my own. Empathy consists of never losing sight of this and therefore always being conscious of the way in which I position myself in the world of the other person, rather than only paying attention to the way in which the other person is positioned in my own world. This perpetual attention to empathy is something I find in Alejandro's behavior. Perhaps his goodness is an aspect of this empathy.

What you call empathy is a non-egocentric perspective?

That's right. On the one hand recognizing one's "centrism" around oneself, while also recognizing the other person's right to centrism around himself. And in this way situating oneself in relations "from world to world": How does my world enter into yours? What precautions must I take in order not to shock your world? If I come to you with an extraordinarily present world, how do I not encroach too much on your world? I think Alejandro is extremely conscious of this "world to world" interplay.

I suppose that this empathy comes out in the process of artistic collaboration?

Absolutely, and very strongly. As I said he never likes to press his own universe upon another person's art. He always considers the specific world of the person he is collaborating with, in order to truly realize a joint work, with complete honesty. It is a masculine-feminine relationship in two senses. I mean by this that Jodorowsky inseminates the illustrator, who does the same with him in return, rather than working in a unidirectional manner in which the storyline writer merely inoculates his universe into the illustrator, who must then become his graphic womb. For example, Alejandro has a vision of a character and his movements; at this point the illustrator shows him that this character cannot move in this way in this scenery. So Jodorowsky modifies his character according to the artist's suggestions. It's like internal cooking that takes place in a perpetual exchange. Each person alternates in taking on the masculine and feminine roles in total fluidity. Alejandro perceives the creative potential of the illustrator and knows how to guide it into the scenario, which is not envisaged as something immutable.

Do you have a story to share along these lines?

There are plenty, evidently. Here is a recent one. I was working with him on volume III of the *Bouncer* series. At a certain moment there is an exchange between the heroes—the Bouncer, who is missing an arm, and a Black, who is going to kidnap his fiancée. To have someone to talk to, this Black, who is a solitary character, owns a dog. I say to myself: "Hmm, I'm going to draw a dog that is missing one paw." I propose the idea to Alejandro, who picks it up and goes on from there.

There comes a moment in the story when the Black goes off with the Bouncer's girlfriend and leaves him his dog. So there's a dog missing one paw accompanying a character who is missing an arm. Then we start to envisage the fourth volume, which will conclude the series, and I say to Alejandro: "You know, we could do something great and terrible: the dog saves the Bouncer's life, but in doing so, has to die." And Alejandro reacts immediately: "What? Kill a dog? Impossible, out of the question!"

"Listen, Alejandro, we kill people all throughout the pages of this series, but you don't want to sacrifice one dog?"

"No, no, we can't do that, it's too terrible."

Seeing his resistance, I give up: "Okay, you don't want us to kill the dog, he can live . . ."

A month later he calls me and says:

"You know, they're reprinting my novel *Le Paradis des perroquets,* and I've just received an archived copy of the first edition ever. And do you know what? In this novel there is a dog with three paws! So this dog represents my first novel. Now I understand why I can't kill it!"

These things may seem trifling, but they constantly pave the way for an artistic collaboration, and they keep us perpetually in a sort of state of exaltation. We have experienced this kind of synchronicity for some fifteen years now.

Alejandro is someone who is known, admired, a reference-point for many people and in many fields: BD, film, spirituality, tarot, literature. The fact that he can also "be one with" others, to borrow an expression from Swami Prajnanpad, in communion with the world of the other person, suggests that he does not identify too much with himself.

Absolutely. I am always amazed when I find Alejandro in the café with this whole world of people who surround him and expect so many things from him.

How do you mean, amazed?

It is not at all the same relationship that we have from day to day when we are working on a *bande dessinée.* Sometimes we just say things like, "Okay, here, how is the guy going to draw his revolver? Will he do it like this or like that?" We are completely taken up in the adventure we are creating. And then I see him with people who hang on his least gesture, who idealize him wholesale. Now, I know he transitions easily from one situation into another. I have the impression that he completely accepts all the projections people make on him, but without adhering to any of them. He is almost amused by them. Then he goes home, continues with his artistic creation, and persists in his desire to write and make BDs. He has great freedom precisely because he remains in a state of non-identification, of distancing, that allows him total leeway for undertaking things and for living.

All in all these are suppositions on my part, I do not live under his skin; but in any case this is what I sense from contact with him.

What would you say about his relationship with bandes dessinées? It's a genre to which he came rather late in life.
Around the age of fifty, I think.

As an illustrator who is completely invested in BD, how do you view your relationship with this "ninth art"? For example, I never hear him speak of bandes dessinées; he uses the American term "comics," which brings to mind American "comic strips," published without any pretense in newspapers.

In fact, I think he has a very high opinion of BD. He is a tarologist. As such he has such great appreciation for imagery, such knowledge of the images of the tarot, that he must by necessity see the same ambition in the realm of BD. Of course this ambition is not always supported by knowledge comparable to that of the medieval artists; it all depends on the illustrators. The fact remains that he has created complicity between the world of BD and the symbolic world of the tarot. Alejandro is, without doubt, a writer, but he is also very visual. In addition to his writing, he has all the possibilities of design and the visual arts.

He is a filmmaker, and BD is the art closest to film.

Indeed! So even if he uses the term "comics," which refers to a minor art, he cannot be unaware, having worked with so many masters of the genre, that BD is an art in its own right and that an extraordinary level of knowledge is present in the practice of an illustrator, sometimes unbeknown to the artist himself. We manipulate representations of the world, the human being, scenes that sometimes date back thousands of years. It's a culture that spans centuries and is enriched with every new representation. I believe Alejandro is very conscious of this.

As you have just mentioned, Alejandro, as a story writer, has worked with many of the uncontested masters of the genre: Mœbius, Bess, the late Arno, Gimenez, Janjetov, Baltran, and others still, as well as—not to affront your modesty—François Boucq. The series he has created have become downright mythical: Moon Face, The Incal, John Difool, The White Llama, Aleph Tau, The Metabarons, to name but a few. . . . He sets the standard for BD fans, who most likely do not know the other facets of his personality. One could therefore say that he is greatly respected in the world of what he calls "comics." However, I can't believe that the other dimension he operates in does not provoke resistance. What sort of reputation does he have in the BD milieu, among the professionals who do not share in his quest?

You are right to point this out. Many of those who have not worked with him have a negative idea of Alejandro. In my view this comes from a misinterpretation of what he is, of his creations, of things he may have said. He is often seen as a "guru" in the negative sense of the word, a manipulator, an illusionist who lives off of other artists. To me this seems to come from misunderstanding and also from a certain uneasiness, a fear like what one might feel when standing on a dock at a port, looking at the ocean, wondering whether one dares to depart or not. Sometimes artistic creation turns into risk-taking, when one is facing a turning point. Now, many illustrators have a tendency to become frozen in a world of nostalgia, the *bandes dessinées* of their childhoods, things they already know. They rehash *The Lord of the Rings* for the umpteenth time. I remember the creation of *Moon Face;* I wondered how I could draw a world constantly devastated by waves. I almost felt anguish, faced with the task of depicting such an evanescent universe. This required a sort of temerity, unconsciousness, and pleasure at discovering an unknown world. Not everyone is ready to take this sort of risk.

But one cannot deny the fact that great illustrators such as those you have mentioned have also invested in Alejandro all along. For those who dare he sparks a rebirth, a constant expansion; he breaks down barriers.

Did the illustrators who worked with Jodo form a kind of fellowship? I remember meeting you, along with Mœbius, at Alejandro's house in Vincennes. Jean Annestay was also there.

There was not any fellowship that met formally or regularly. I had a very good relationship with Giraud and Mœbius. We met several times with Bess, especially at Alejandro's lectures, but without ever becoming close. As for Arno he died relatively early on. At the time when I started working with Alejandro, Arno was already near the end. By contrast I recently met Gimenez, who has a different kind of relationship with Jodo. It's as if there's a constant arm-wrestling match going on between them. Moreover, it's interesting to see the different relationships he has with each illustrator. Gimenez is a bit like a mischievous gnome who tries to provoke Jodo. I may be wrong about this, but it seems that Gimenez feels he is facing an authority figure whom he attempts to destabilize with pranks. So, there is no formal fellowship. Perhaps a subtle fellowship.

Finally what would you say today about your relationship with Jodorowsky, more than fifteen years after it began?

It is difficult to describe it in only a few words. It's a relationship made up of many elements that have bound us together closely . . .

At the beginning, you spoke of your reputation as an illustrator who quarrels with his story writers. Do you feel that you could quarrel with Alejandro?

Without doubt we could have quarreled plenty of times! But we maintained our good relationship, and therefore we tried to dispel any potential quarrels at the moment they arose. Every relationship, ultimately, can be destroyed at any moment, under any pretext. There are plenty of points at which a joint artistic creation carried on by two people can break apart, perhaps more so than any other kind of relationship. But that is the test that allows one to see to what point the relationship will continue. What makes me happy is to see how much we each want to preserve this relationship. A relationship ceases when it becomes sterile; but we know that our relationship can still bear many fruits.

NINE

A GREAT SENSE
OF CLOSENESS
Interview with
Arnaud Desjardins

Born in 1925 Arnaud Desjardins worked as a producer for French public television (formerly ORTF) until 1973. While producing a number of popular TV shows, he became familiar with the living spiritualities of Asia through a series of documentaries. A member of the French Society of Great Voyagers and Explorers, he travels by car—sometimes accompanied by his wife and their two children—without a film crew, with only one 16-millimeter camera, his film reels, and his sound and light systems, sometimes staying a long time before starting to film with the masters and disciples who receive him. This working method allows him to produce films that remain today as exceptional documentation of the Hindu ashrams, the Sufis of Afghanistan, Tibetan Buddhism, and Japanese Zen. Following his personal quest hand in hand with his filmmaking career, he became the disciple of a Hindu spiritual master who was unknown at the time, Shri Swami Prajnanpad, with whom he stayed regularly. In 1974 he abandoned television and, in cooperation with his master, founded a small ashram in the heart of Auvergne: Le Bost, intended to receive a limited number of participants. The books he published about the teachings he had received drew more and more people, wishing to explore this path. In 1983 he left Le Bost and opened a new ashram in Gard: Font d'Isière. In 1995 he opened Hauteville, a large spiritual center located in Ardèche.

Today he is known for being one of the major spokespeople of a living and open spirituality in the francophone world. He has published about twenty authoritative works.

I only had to take a few steps to meet with Arnaud, leaving my interview room in Hauteville, climbing the great staircase, and walking down the hallway that led to his, where I and many other people had gone through memorable moments.

And I will say only one thing, at the risk of aggravating those who are unaware that this man is a true spiritual guide and who see only infantilism, even idolatry, there: to stand in this room in the presence of Arnaud Desjardins, even if the topic at hand was not myself but Jodorowsky, was to be in the presence of a man who, with age and experience, is approaching closer and closer to the essential nature of things.

However unassuming he may be, one leaves this place nourished, suffused with an unusual kind of atmosphere. Sitting on his bed, surrounded by mystic books and photographs of the sages who have enlightened his life, Arnaud Desjardins, at the age of seventy-eight, starts with an exercise of admiration.

What strikes me most about Jodorowsky is his originality; not in the condescending sense of the term, when one says "he's an original" meaning that the person is a bit maladjusted or is seeking to be noticed by any means possible. Jodorowsky is an original in that he is totally himself, unique, not imitating anyone. His singularity lies in his natural expression and simply in what he is. Moreover, and this is very remarkable, he manages to be totally himself, original, in many different domains.

He may have had an international career as a filmmaker; but although he has made some striking films—I myself have seen *Holy Mountain* and *Tusk,* and they both made a strong impression—he cannot be simply categorized as a filmmaker. He may have had a career as a tarologist and therapist, a career as a writer, a career as a theater director, a career as a story writer for *bandes dessinées.* In fact, one might say that he has, or has had, each of these careers, but without letting himself be reduced to one or the other of them, never falling into the trap of spreading himself too thin or becoming superficial. And this is very surprising: he does many things, but everything he does, he does well, at full throttle, completely. I admire him all the more because I, through my temperament and education, was led to explore a single domain, seeking to be an honest work-man. One might say this is a classical framework in which it is important to be successful. It is true that I have led a very varied life. I first earned my own money at the age of nineteen, after the war, imitating the stars of the era in a small cabaret, while also pursuing self-taught studies in theology and phi-losophy after Sciences Po. I created all sorts of TV shows, not just films about spiritual traditions. So I no longer followed a very conventional path. But even for someone like me, whose human experience has been rather broad, Jodorowsky's "case," if you will, remains striking. He is astounding, an extremely rare example by reason of his many talents and the use he makes of them. And I haven't even mentioned his contacts with shamans and sorcerers in Mexico and elsewhere. This is why I sometimes say that he is perhaps the only person about whom I feel unable to be completely objective, so amazing he appears to me.

I must also mention his goodness, his way of being attentive to others. His "Mystic Cabarets," his tarot readings, are notorious events, but not the only ones, in which he expresses this goodness, which touches me—I who sometimes say I would like my epitaph to say: "He was a nice guy."

Do you remember your first meetings with him?

Yes, certainly, at your house then at a restaurant. I knew that I was going to meet an international filmmaker. Through my professional career I was a priori impressed by filmmakers who have directed major films. I must say that at this time I was not familiar with the other sides of Alejandro, having not read *La Tricherie sacrée,* which had just been published. But I was immediately struck by his extremely unassuming nature, a very rare characteristic for anyone who has achieved success and fame. In general someone who has been successful becomes to some extent a prisoner of his personality. If you meet someone at a party who is distinguished in his field, he will make sure to let you know very quickly, within the first few minutes of conversation—and even if he is a nice person—that you are in the presence of a great surgeon, a famous film director, a well-known writer, a famous journalist. I remember that I had to make an effort to remember that this man, so authentically unassuming, who came to me without any pretension—rather, if you will, as someone interested in India who had been invited to dinner along with me—was someone famous, an artist with an international reputation, not to mention his other equally recognized talents. This impression was repeated every time I met with him.

Like all the people I have asked to talk about him for this new edition of La Tricherie sacrée, you have mentioned his goodness.

Ah yes, he has a great sense of his fellow beings. Wherever he goes he is not content with just showing what he knows how to do, but manifests a true goodness, a real interest in other people. Through his non-identification with his own personality and his attention to others, he bears witness to a lifelong spirituality that impresses me; that I take very seriously.

Can you explain what you mean by "non-identification with his own personality"?

In fact, even though I feel close to him, I have not met Alejandro very often. In fifteen years we have only seen each other a few times and in very different contexts each time. At friends' houses; at a restaurant; at the *Maison de la Poésie,* where, at the request of my son, who was working there, we held a party in honor of René Daumal; and here in Hauteville, where I invited him to speak before our annual general assembly, which is a chance for various spokespeople of current spiritualities to share their experience with our attendees. What struck me each time was his way of adapting himself, of taking stock of the situation as a whole. Many people, if one observes them closely, have difficulty getting out of their own personalities—including, alas, their personality of spiritual teacher, if such is the case. One of the real and visible signs of human and spiritual maturity is this ability to adapt, this sense of the other person, of the context, while also remaining completely loyal to oneself.

He never strikes the wrong note. He adapts very respectfully to the context, to the environment. For all that one could say that Jodorowsky is a "personality," he does not have a fixed "Jodo personality" that he broadcasts and imposes wherever he goes. He adapted perfectly to Hauteville and to the other very diverse participants. He knows how to be present with other people, and his tone is always correct. For me this is very persuasive. This is someone who is very sure of himself, but who is never encumbered by his ego.

You told me you greatly appreciated his book Gospels to Heal.

Very much, indeed. I understand that this book can unsettle and even shock those who misunderstand the intention from which it proceeds. As far as I am concerned, it is a totally original and unique book on a subject that has been abundantly written about—the Gospels—where Jodorowsky shows us Mary both as the mother of Christ and as a woman in her own right. Regarding Mary he speaks magnificently of the woman and develops ideas that might well reach contemporary women. This book, in a certain way, is frightening, disconcerting, rattling, stamped with a great purity, a very profound understanding, in my view, of the Gospels as a mystic text. An inimitable alloy of extreme boldness and great humility, just like its author, this book nourished me personally. I have just read its second volume, *The Inner God,* and I was in no way disappointed. I found that depth there, which dares anything but whose audacity is never gratuitous.

Arnaud, I conclude from this that you are a fan of Jodorowsky.
You can say it that way if you like! In fact, I'll say it again: he demonstrates to me a living and authentic spirituality. I consider him one of the great spokespeople of this dimension in the twentieth century and the beginning of the twenty-first century.

He is a man outside of any category, certainly one of the greatest encounters that life has brought me in this last episode of my existence.

TEN

A LETTER
FROM YOUR SON
Adan Jodorowsky

Dear Father, Alejandro,

You that always thought that calling "dad" to a father is a mistake. That "dad" and "mom" are the first words that a baby can say and calling them like that being an adult, means to keep a son prisoner as a child. You, that told me, "I'm not Dad, my name is Alejandro; I don't call you adad, dada, or adadá . . ."

I write this letter publicly because I want the world to know that the love between a father and a son exists. I see so many cases of absent fathers or those who don't accept their children as they are. That is why today I want everybody to know how a real relationship of love and respect can be. I hope it serves as an example for the planet in order to make a positive transformation and stop creating wars, which are consequences of suppressed anger.

Calling you Alejandro didn't make me miss anything. On the contrary I didn't see you as an emblematic figure or as a superior being. I saw you as an ally: a being full of kindness.

Calling you Alejandro is the most tender and wonderful thing in the world. And the fact I felt different from the other kids, caused me a great sense of strength.

You never educated me with fear; you never hit me. You talked to me, explained everything, and took care of teaching me your thoughts, leaving me free to be the one I had to be and not who you wanted me to be. Do you remember? You used to sit down next to me and read Japanese tales to initiate me into a life philosophy.

You've formed my mind and trained me like a warrior to receive the blows of life, to receive stupid speeches, to receive the human imbecility. But you also taught me to recognize the beauty inside the ugliness.

I remember one day you said to me, "I'm going to teach you to think." We were in Spain, spending our holidays on an island, and every morning you gave me lessons to think. Every father should teach his son to think. Children aren't dumb; they're like sponges, and what you teach them will remain for their whole life, and they need it. Thanks to this you marked me forever. "What is God? What is the universe? Which is our purpose here? Where did I come from? Where will I go? Am I a body with a soul or soul with a body? Your truth is a truth but not the truth."

You taught me to speak as a conscious and delicate person. When I was a child you spoke to me softly, but as an adult you didn't infantilize me with cartoon voices. Parents usually speak to their children as if they were dolls, but you talked to me as a human being. Then you showed me how to communicate with the others, and instead of making a statement in a conversation, I learned to say before I start a sentence: "According to my opinion and I could be wrong . . ."

In an argument, instead of accusing, you taught me to express how I feel and what caused that discussion in me. You never made me part of your financial concerns, so money was never a problem for me. I've lived in a paradise. A child has to see life as a paradise. The opposite turns one into a distressed being, fearful to face its existence.

When I was angry, instead of making me hold it, you took my hand, we went to the garden, and you made me destroy a chair into a thousand pieces. You can't imagine the happiness that meant to me to destroy that poor chair. I told you: "But if I break it we'll no longer have the chair. . . ." And you answered it didn't matter; you would buy another. For you the material matter had no importance. The only value that you saw was in the human being.

Instead of suppressing my creativity, you bought me brushes so I could paint on the walls of my room. Nothing was forbidden to me. Whenever I made a mistake, we talked about it and fixed it. You trusted in me and in the limits that I imposed on myself. I could do and ask everything. I was a child, and we talked openly about sex without a religious moral that could make me believe it was something insane. When someone had sex in the house, the next day was celebrated.

When I wanted an instrument, instead of thinking it was a whim, you bought me a piano, a trumpet, even if I used it for a day. You said that everything is useful in life. And it's true; everything I asked and you gave me in my childhood helped me. Absolutely everything. You never put any limit on my creativity. You taught me how to meditate; you gave me books.

Although you and my mother separated when I was eight years old, you never spoke to me in a bad way about her. You

*didn't try to destroy my love for her. And you created a love
relationship between my brothers and me, without competition,
loving each one differently.*

*You taught me to believe that everything is possible in life.
And how? I will remind you how: One day we were wandering
around the streets of Paris looking for a pair of shoes, and until
I'd find the perfect ones, we weren't going to surrender. We went
to fifteen stores until we found what I really wanted. Thank you,
father of my heart; thanks to it nowadays, until I'm satisfied with
what I'm creating, I don't quit. Also, you taught me that when
something isn't achieved, there are other ways that can lead us
to our wishes.*

*When I stumbled on the street, you said to me "Samurai!"
in order to be conscious of each step, each look of mine into the
world. The Samurai is never distracted. I feel alive, Alejandro,
so alive. I never saw you depressed. Do you realize? You never
complained or let yourself be overcome by the weight of life. You
never showed me your anxieties. You taught me to be happy,
to think that life is a party. You taught me not to smoke when
the teenagers started doing it. You explained to me that I was a
confident kid, and I didn't need a cigarette to be seduced or be
accepted by others. I felt strong, so strong. You taught me to love
myself and to respect my temple, my body.*

*I watched you writing eight hours a day, your whole life
dedicated to your art. You've found true love at the age of seventy-
five. You met your wife, Pascale, and it's the most beautiful story
I've ever seen in my life. You made me believe in the union of two
souls. Now I have faith in love at any age.*

*Sometimes you ask me: "How do you feel mentally, physically,
sexually, emotionally?" You communicate with my whole being.*

When I come to your house, I sit in front of you and you look at me, you tell me your life and ask about mine, and we try to make our monologues last the same amount of time, so we have a balanced conversation, and no one speaks more than the other.

You worry for me without invading my space. But you always tell me that you love me. Every parent should say it to his son.

When I was a child and you had to travel, you called me every day, even if it was for two minutes. That was our deal. I felt your presence. I always felt that I could count on you. Every time you said something, you accomplished it. And the most important thing for a child is that a father keeps his promises. Once I went on vacation with the school, and I felt so bad with the children, I felt so different from them that I called you crying. That same night you came with your car. You drove 250 miles to get me out of hell. And we came back together, singing. You said a child should not suffer because the early years are sacred.

You always smelled my hair and my skin saying I smelled marvelously well. You always told me that I had talent, that I was beautiful, that I was a prince. You caressed me, touched me, hugged me. I was loved. In the morning I knocked on your door and ran into bed next to you so you hugged me. With my head on your breast, I listened to your breathing and your heart beating. Then we used to have breakfast in a café in front of our house, and you talked to me about books, movies, about the discoveries that you made, about the new spiritual ideas that you had thought.

At this moment I'm crying out of emotion because I had never taken the time to tell you all this. You're a wonderful father. My tears run; those tears are drops of love.

You always took me with you to your conferences, your seminars, I saw you healing people, giving them smiles, calming fears. We have collaborated in theater, in cinema, in my songs. How wonderful it is to be able to create something with your family.

When I had a doubt, you were always present. So present that if you weren't on my side today, I would still listen to your voice in my mind, advising me. I have you tattooed on me, forever.

You saved me, Alejandro, from this cruel world, from this chaos that is life. You showed me the most beautiful thing of all. You kept me away from bourgeois thoughts, illusions, religious thinking. You taught me to have no limits. You taught me that I'm a free man. Free from human madness, free of wars, of fears. You taught me that the reality where we live is not the only reality. There are no limits; my territory is not a house, a country, or a world, but the entire universe, the infinity.

Why did you let me paint on the walls of my room? I have wondered so much. Why give me the freedom to do what I wanted? I understood that you were teaching me to create, to free my mind, to live without restrictions, without walls. Those walls were illusory, invisible, and by painting them I could pass through them.

You taught me to talk: not too little, not too much. You taught me to respect the energy fields of others. You taught me to count on the tarot cards. And you showed me that symbols are art. You taught me that life is magic and that the miracles are everywhere. You taught me that God is an energy that lives in us and not a severe being made up by writers. You opened an account for me at a bookshop, and thanks to you I discovered poetry. Poetry! I remember we sat at the dining room table, and each of us read his poem.

You never had useless friends; the only people who entered into our house were the ones that you wanted to help or people with talent: poets, philosophers, singers, doctors, shoemakers, saints, all kinds of people but with soul and content. You never wasted your time on empty conversations. I've never seen you drunk or drugged. I only saw you develop your mind and your talent in a positive way in order to change the world and bring something to it.

For many years you felt a failed writer, and look what you've done. At the age of sixty, you freed yourself of that feeling and published more than thirty books. Today you are eighty-five years old and you're such a successful writer. All that because you believe in yourself. What an example. How many people do not believe in what they are and look for a way out, being unable to see that everything is vibrating in them from the beginning?

You talked to me about aging as something beautiful, and thanks to you I enjoy each year with no fear of death. Thanks to you I know that everything is possible in this life, at any time.

I see the love in your eyes when you look at me. You loved me and gave me so much that I love you without boundaries. You created the being that is writing now. You created my love for you. You perfectly applied that sentence you wrote, and it turned out to be so true. What you give, you give it to yourself; what you don't give, you take it away from yourself.

Thank you for giving me this life.

Your son Adan who loves you

A Little Act
of Goodness

It is teatime at Jodo's apartment. The whole family is together in the living room. Adan, in a corner, flips through *bandes dessinées,* the master is in his armchair by the window, Marianne is participating in the conversation while also answering e-mails concerning Alejandro on her laptop. First there is a request from a video producer in the United States, asking if he can publish a laudatory quote from Jodorowsky in his catalog. Alejandro is willing, as long as he can use the term "porn" in the series of favorable adjectives. "These videos are not just marvelous, they are also sometimes porn, yes? So, if we say 'porn,' I'll do it . . ."

Then there is the question of Allen Klein—yes, the infamous ex-manager of the Beatles and the Rolling Stones, mentioned by Philippe Manœuvre, the dark side of rock and roll who still holds the rights to films by Jodorowsky and, in fact, prevents us from seeing them on DVD—with the exception of *Santa Sangre* and Alejandro's first film ever, *Fando and Lis,* recently rereleased with a bonus documentary by Emmanuel Mouchet, which shows Jodo in Vincennes during the era of *La Tricherie sacrée*.

Alejandro and Marianne have a meeting in London the next day with Mr. Klein, in what I understand to be a spirit of reconciliation.

"Aaaaah, I am so happy. You don't know how sweet it is to make peace with old enemies. We talked on the telephone, yes; we were like old wrestlers who have fought and are happy to see each other again. He told me: 'Ah, that was a good time, we did great things.'"

While Alejandro is saying this, the telephone rings: "Ah yes, I do not speak English so well, you talk to my wife." Marianne takes the telephone; it is Klein's secretary, confirming their appointment.

There is also a poet there, Emmanuel Lequeux, the brave leader of a small publishing house, Le Veilleur, which publishes poems by Alejandro and, soon, a collection by Marianne. She is currently in contact with the old beat poet Lawrence Ferlinghetti, and now we begin talking about Allen Ginsberg: in fact, I am about to publish a book in which I share memories of my conversations and meetings with him. When any major artistic figure of the 1960s or 1970s is mentioned, it is rare for Alejandro not to have known him or her. At the moment he reminisces about his contacts with the author of *Howl:* "In Paris he came to see me, telling me 'I am looking for an angel.' He asked me to take him to a gay club. At the time there were not many of them, and in any case I only knew about one. I took him there; it was on the third floor. I was still a handsome man then, and I found myself in this place full of homosexuals looking at me. I left him there;

later I saw him in New York; he lived with a crazy guy, yes?

"Well, I was so absorbed in myself at that time that I did not really pay attention, but yes, I met him, Ginsberg."

Alejandro then shows me a book of photos of mysterious crop circles, immense and very elaborate, which seem to form all on their own in fields, especially in England.

And we talk a little more, initially with Jodorowsky in the role of questioner.

Jodorowsky: All right, Gilles. . . . Once there was a man who was almost old and a man who was almost young. We were not the same. Your spirit is not the same. When you were young you were curious, you were searching for something, or rather you felt that something was searching for you, and you were not really sure what it was. And then, when one becomes an adult, as you have become, one knows. You know what you are lacking, but you also know what is searching for you and why you do things. You do not grope around like you used to. So it would be interesting if you would tell my why you have returned to *La Tricherie sacrée*. . . .You have known plenty of highly evolved people, you have done a lot of things, you have worked with Arnaud Desjardins. What will this do for you? What will this do for us?

Farcet: First of all, Alejandro, it's life that has brought it about, in the form of the publisher, Dervy. There is a demand to which we answer yes. It's true, today I no longer feel the same need to explore, to encounter, at least not in the same way. My path is more focused. At the age of twenty-nine, meeting Jodorowsky, getting to know him, collaborating with him on two books:

that was part of my construction. Today, apparently, I could pass it up. At the same time, on a personal level, what a lesson it is to see a man like you evolve, continue to mature, to grow, to learn. And what a gift it is to meet the people who I asked to talk about you, about the ways in which you touched each of them. For me this is a beautiful lesson about humanity. So as far as I am concerned, returning to *La Tricherie* is a lesson for me, not to mention the pleasure of spending time with you. As for you I do not know how it will serve you. Perhaps, when you reread our interviews, it will allow you to take stock of your evolution. Without a doubt you will be touched by the testimonies of these six people—and there could have been many others—who you have influenced and who love you. But above all, beyond our personalities, yours and mine, I believe that this book can be useful as a testimony to the evolution of a consciousness. I see it as a useful book dedicated to a useful being.

Jodorowsky: What you say inspires me in many ways: First, when life proposes something, it is a challenge. At a given moment, in a state of meditation, we can feel that we do not need anything, that everything is within ourselves. So why move? But luckily life offers us challenges. The mosquito that bit Buddha was a challenge for Buddha. But I am not Buddha, and neither are you.

Farcet: Much less!

Jodorowsky: But even still a challenge like this makes us come out of our meditation. It makes you leave Hauteville, eh? There is a haiku I like, which says that the cloud that hides the moon allows me to rest. Sometimes we can be in the inner light, and the cloud comes to distract us and offer us a break. This is an amusement, a game. A useful game.

I still have an ego, you know.

Farcet: In case anyone might doubt it, so do I.

Jodorowsky: But I do not believe one can separate from the ego. One can tame it.

Farcet: One can put it in its place.

Jodorowsky: Right! Now, as for me, I must say—even if there is a power that holds me back a little from saying it—that I am involved more and more on the path of goodness.

Farcet: That's the keyword, Alejandro, goodness. The word that keeps coming from the mouths of all those who speak of you.

Jodorowsky: I will tell you about an act of goodness that I carried out, at the risk of seeming vain, because it is true that most of the time one must not talk about one's acts of goodness. I pursue my investigation of goodness because it was one of my characteristics when I was a child: I was good. When I see a person come to me, I put myself into a state of goodness. You see, today I spent time with someone who was a little depressed, and I put myself into a state of goodness in order to try to help her come out of it. Why do this?

Simply for goodness. There is no other explanation. Likewise, the café where I read the tarot, Le Téméraire, was bought by young Arabs. They arranged it as best they could. When I went to see, I asked them: "Why don't you put mirrors at the back? That will create an impression of depth; your space will be doubled. . . ." And they answered, "That's expensive. It will cost several thousand francs, hundreds of Euros." And suddenly I told them: "I'll make you a present of it!" And I bought them the mirrors. That's madness! As far as I'm concerned, it's not my café, even if they welcome me there every week. But this was of service to me, because now I have the impression that I can contribute to changing the reality of the neighborhood. Now the café is very nice; the people who go there are more pleasant; there is an improvement, a sort of mutation. Later I saw that the young Arab man who runs the café was not very happy, and I asked him if he did any reading. He replied: "No, I don't have time." I told him: "Listen, I'll bring you some comics." Then he told me he preferred films, and I brought him videos. Now he greets me and asks for a psychomagical act. There! Another advance in the neighborhood! You have seen the restaurant across the street where I just lunched with Marianne, Adan, and Coralie? One day I sent them a CD of a singer who had come to see me, Arthur H. They were very happy. Another advance in the neighborhood! These are the little advances that I endeavor to make in the neighborhood. One cannot change the world, but one can begin to change it with little acts of goodness. I wrote a poem about this called *Little Acts of Goodness*. I will read it to you:

Nothing remains for me but to rejoice
To offer the beggar a glass of wine
To stop the cats from pissing on the flowers
To accompany the blind man like a silent dog
To give the lunatic clean sheets
To applaud the bad comedian
To lend money to the swindler
To send roses to the ugly girl
To give my cane to the blind man
Little acts of goodness
Subject to the indifference of a God
Incapable of telling good from evil,
The light of his shadow.

At heart that is what interests me. Even if God is indifferent, I, as a good being, can accomplish acts of goodness, not giving a damn that the world is unjust. What do injustice and vileness matter? I want to do acts of goodness freely, without any reason. One can work a lot on oneself, relying on one center or another: mental, emotional, physical. Consider the case of Jean-Pierre Vignaud, the karate master: he learned everything based on the physical center, nothing mental. All paths lead to Rome, which is to say, to love.

Farcet: Making this book is a little bit like that, isn't it? A little act of goodness . . .

Jodorowsky: Yes! That's right! Ha ha ha!

INDEX

BOOKS OF RELATED INTEREST

Psychomagic
The Transformative Power of Shamanic Psychotherapy
by Alejandro Jodorowsky

Manual of Psychomagic
The Practice of Shamanic Psychotherapy
by Alejandro Jodorowsky

The Dance of Reality
A Psychomagical Autobiography
by Alejandro Jodorowsky

Metagenealogy
Self-Discovery through Psychomagic and the Family Tree
by Alejandro Jodorowsky and Marianne Costa

The Way of Tarot
The Spiritual Teacher in the Cards
by Alejandro Jodorowsky and Marianne Costa

The Spiritual Journey of Alejandro Jodorowsky
The Creator of *El Topo*
by Alejandro Jodorowsky

Visionary Ayahuasca
A Manual for Therapeutic and Spiritual Journeys
by Jan Kounen
Foreword by Alejandro Jodorowsky

Shamanic Transformations
True Stories of the Moment of Awakening
by Itzhak Beery

INNER TRADITIONS • BEAR & COMPANY
P.O. Box 388
Rochester, VT 05767
1-800-246-8648
www.InnerTraditions.com

Or contact your local bookseller